**W9-CFU-530**

GARLAND STUDIES IN

# ENTREPRENEURSHIP

*edited by*
STUART BRUCHEY
ALLAN NEVINS PROFESSOR EMERITUS
COLUMBIA UNIVERSITY

*A GARLAND SERIES*

# THE FORMATION OF ENTREPRENEURIAL INTENTIONS

David F. Summers

GARLAND PUBLISHING, INC.
A MEMBER OF THE TAYLOR & FRANCIS GROUP
NEW YORK & LONDON/2000

Published in 2000 by
Garland Publishing, Inc.
A member of the Taylor & Francis Group
29 West 35th Street
New York, NY 10001

10  9  8  7  6  5  4  3  2  1

*Library of Congress Cataloging-in-Publication Data*
Summers, David F., 1948–
    The formation of entrepreneurial intentions / David F.
Summers
       p. cm. — (Garland studies in entrepreneurship)
    Includes bibliographical references and index.
    ISBN 0-8153-3733-7 (alk. paper)
     1. Entrepreneurship.   I. Title.   II. Series.

HB615 .S953 2000
658.4'21—dc21
                                                   00-026418

Printed on acid-free, 250 year-life paper
Manufactured in the United States of America

# Table of Contents

# Preface

For over twenty years I have been fascinated with the idea of being an entrepreneur. I have owned my own wholesale and retail merchandising firm, been an independent real estate agent, developed a management consulting business, and taught "would be" entrepreneurs the joy and skills of starting a business. In all these years, however, I never really knew why someone would choose to be in business for themselves. For me, the thought of being independent and the chance to build something of value combined with a unique set of life's circumstances influenced my decision. I wanted to know if others felt the same way. This desire led me to focus my dissertation on finding out what personal and situational factors most influence the entrepreneurial decision.

The basic research model for the dissertation was based on the logic of my own experience that people would start a business if they first thought that starting a business was a good idea. Second, they thought that they had the necessary skills, knowledge, ability, opportunity, and resources to be successful. Third, they were willing to take action to get what they wanted. And, finally, they had some event take place in their life that ultimately triggered the decision. The research focused on one hundred and twenty five individuals in which about half were in the process of making the entrepreneurial decision to become independent real estate agents and half were seeking career advancement in non-entrepreneurial avenues. The overall findings supported the underlying logic of the research model.

The research suggested that people formed the intentions to start a firm when they had a positive attitude toward entrepreneurship. Positive attitudes were enhanced by encouraging support from people important to the potential entrepreneur such as family, friends, and mentors. In addition, positive past entrepreneurial experiences fostered positive attitudes. People were also more likely to form intentions to start a firm if they thought they had the necessary skills, ability, knowledge, opportunity, and resources. The research confirmed that people who were inclined to take action to control their environment so they could get what they wanted were likely to start new businesses. Finally, the entrepreneurial decision is often triggered by some life changing event, such the loss of a job, marriage, or just the realization that the career had stalled.

In the final analysis, I learned that most entrepreneurs are just like me and want to start a business for the same reasons. Knowing this helps me encourage others to follow my footsteps and discover the thrill of entrepreneurship.

# Acknowledgements

While only one name appears as the author of this work, it would not have been possible without the support of many individuals. I want to express my appreciation to Dr. Vicki Goodwin who served as the chairman of this project. Her drive for excellence coupled with an unselfish dedication to the completion of this work have been an inspiration to me and something I want to emulate in my career. Thanks goes to committee members Dr. Nancy Boyd and Dr. Alan Kvanli who provided input that greatly added to the value and quality of this work.

This project would not have been possible without the encouragement and support of Dr. Winston Stahlecker, former head of the Department of Management, Marketing, and General Business at West Texas A&M University. I would also like to thank the my other colleagues at West Texas A&M University who kept telling me that "it's all worth it." I needed the encouragement from time to time.

I want to recognize my mother, Louise Summers, who always wanted the best for her children, and worked so hard to provide it. Most importantly, I want to thank my wife, Cynthia and son, John who have sacrificed much and, thus, given me the inspiration to complete this dissertation. It is to them that I lovingly dedicate this work.

# List of Tables

# List of Figures

# THE FORMATION OF ENTREPRENEURIAL INTENTIONS

## CHAPTER I

# Introduction

The need to understand entrepreneurship has never been more important than it is today (Bygrave, 1993, p.256). In the United States alone, entrepreneurial activity accounts for 38 percent of the gross domestic product and 40 to 80 percent of all new jobs (Dennis, 1993). This significant economic impact has fueled the current interest in research of the entrepreneurial phenomenon.

In spite of growing interest in entrepreneurship, little consensus exists among researchers concerning entrepreneurial theories, definitions, and research directions (Bull & Willard, 1993; Carland, Hoy, & Carland 1988; Gartner, 1988; Wortman, 1987). One explanation is that entrepreneurship is a multi-faceted phenomenon that crosses many academic disciplines (Low & MacMillian, 1988). Regardless of the complexity of the phenomenon or research debate, the importance of entrepreneurship demands research attention.

Early research into entrepreneurship and the individual decision to become an entrepreneur has focused primarily on "who entrepreneurs are" (trait approach) or "what entrepreneurs do" (behavior approach) (Gartner, 1988). For example, Boyd and Vozikis (1994) point out that such traits as McClelland's (1961) need for achievement, locus of control (Brockhaus, 1982), risk-taking propensity (Brockhaus, 1980), and tolerance for ambiguity (Schere, 1982) have been associated with entrepreneurship. On the other hand, Gartner (1988) argues that individual traits are ancillary to the entrepreneur's behavior. The focus, therefore, should be on what the entrepreneur does and not who the entrepreneur is. Research by Herbert and Link (1982) and Shapero (1982) has taken a more behavioral approach in explaining how entrepreneurship occurs by focusing on the activities of entrepreneurship (e.g., opportunity recognition, gathering resources). Neither the trait nor the behavior approach alone, however, fully explains the complexity of the entrepreneurial phenomenon.

In an attempt to combine the trait and behavior approaches, expand the research arena, and more accurately capture the complexity of entrepreneurship, researchers have presented comprehensive flow models of the venture creation process (i.e., Behave, 1994; Gartner, 1985; Martin, 1984; Moore, 1986; Vesper, 1980). These process models include a series of critical entrepreneurial behaviors such as opportunity recognition (Behave 1994; Krueger, 1989), firm initiation (Behave, 1994; Martin 1984; Moore, 1986; Shapero, 1982), and firm growth (Moore, 1986). Also included in these models is the influence of personal traits such as those previously mentioned: need for achievement, locus of control, risk taking propensity, and tolerance for ambiguity. Finally, these models consider the roles that personal characteristics (e.g., age, education, gender, minority status) along with social influences (e.g., role models, parents, family, community) and environmental factors (e.g., government influence, capital availability, competition) play in the entrepreneurial process (Gartner, 1985; Martin, 1984; Matthews & Moser, 1996; Moore, 1986).

Regardless of the comprehensiveness or the complexity of the entrepreneurial model, organizations are founded by individuals who make the critical cognitive decision to start the business (Learned, 1992). Each of these individuals brings an accumulation of unique combinations of background and disposition that trigger the decision to start or abort the whole idea of starting a business (Naffziger, Hornsby, & Kuratko, 1994). Not all individuals have the potential for entrepreneurship, and of those who do, not all will attempt the process. Of those who attempt, not all will be successful (Learned, 1992). Therefore, the primary element of entrepreneurship is the critical combination of the individual, his or her past experience, background, and the decision to start an enterprise.

Learned (1992) developed a framework of the founding process that includes the consideration of the individual and his or her experience and background. He proposed that the founding process has four primary dimensions: 1) propensity to found, 2) intention to found, 3) sense making, and 4) the decision to found.

Propensity to found suggests that some individuals have a combination of psychological traits that interact with background factors to make them likely candidates to attempt to start a business. Intention to found posits that some individuals will encounter situations that will interact with their traits and backgrounds to cause the intention to start a business. Sense making implies that intentional individuals interact with the environment while attempting to gather resources and make their business a reality. As a result, intentioned individuals will ultimately make the decision to start a business or abandon the attempt to start depending upon the sense made of the attempt (Learned, 1992).

Critical to Learned's (1992) process is the formation of entrepreneurial intentions. In addition, as Learned (1992) suggested, the formation of intentions is the result of the interaction of psychological traits and background experiences of the individual with situations that are favorable to entrepreneurship. Therefore, the focus of this study is to develop a model that explains the unique combination of the individual entrepreneur and his or her experiences and background that ultimately leads to the formation of entrepreneurial intentions to start a business.

## STATEMENT OF PROBLEM

Intentions have been clearly demonstrated to be the single best predictor of planned behavior (Krueger, 1993). Considering the fact that new entrepreneurial organizations emerge over time as a result of careful thought and action, entrepreneurship is an example of such planned behavior (Bird, 1988; Katz & Gartner, 1988). In addition, entrepreneurship is a process that does not occur in a vacuum but is influenced by a variety of cultural and social factors as well as personal traits and characteristics (Reynolds, 1992). Intentions-based process models are able to capture the complexity of entrepreneurship and provide a framework to build robust, testable process models of entrepreneurship (Krueger, Reilly, & Carsrud, 1995; MacMillian & Katz, 1992).

Researchers have developed several intentions-based models of planned behavior and entrepreneurship such as the theory of planned behavior (Ajzen, 1991; Ajzen & Fishbein, 1980) and Shapero's (1982) model of the entrepreneurial event. Expansions and revisions of intentions models have been proposed by Bird (1988) and Boyd and Vozikis (1994). Despite the interest in intentions-based models, few studies explicitly use theory-driven intentions-based process models of entrepreneurship (Gartner, 1988; Mac-Millian & Katz, 1992). Fewer still include theory-based models of entrepreneurial intentions (Krueger, et al., 1995). The lack of research using intentions-based models is interesting considering that these models have the potential to address the critics of entrepreneurship research who decry that models built from censored samples and from "20-20" hindsight produce spurious results and explanations (Krueger et al., 1995). Therefore, the current study uses an intentions-based model to answer the following research question: "What personal and situational factors relate to the formation of entrepreneurial intentions?"

## PURPOSE OF STUDY

The study was designed to be a theory-building effort in which the relationships among the personal traits and characteristics of the entrepreneur along with predisposing events can be examined for their relationship with the formation of entrepreneurial intentions. The study focused on using a theoretically sound intentions-based process model of entrepreneurship that includes traits and characteristics of the entrepreneur along with predisposing events. The results are used as the first step in predicting entrepreneurial behavior.

The following section provides an overview of the literature that constitutes the theoretical foundation for the study. Work done on previous intentions-based models of entrepreneurship plus research conducted in contexts outside entrepreneurship provide the basis for the research model.

## THEORETICAL FOUNDATION

Central to entrepreneurship is the ultimate decision of the entrepreneur to start the enterprise. Learned (1992) described the starting, or as he put it the founding, process as having four dimensions - 1) propensity to found, 2) intention to found, 3) sense making, and 4) the decision to found. Some individuals have a combination of psychological traits that interact with background factors that give them a propensity to found and, thus, become likely candidates to attempt to start a business. Not all individuals with a propensity to found, however, will develop the intentions to found. Only when individuals encounter situations positively that interact with their traits and background factors, will they develop the intentions to found. Not all intentioned individuals will make the final decision to found. Sense making implies that intentioned individuals interact with the environment while attempting to gather resources and make the business a reality. As a result, intentioned individuals will ultimately make the decision to start a business or abandon the attempt depending upon the sense made of the attempt (Learned, 1992). Based on the discussion of Learned's framework, the formation of entrepreneurial intentions is critical to making the final decision to found the business. Therefore, intentions-based models of entrepreneurship hold significant potential to explain the early entrepreneurial process, even before the firm emerges (Bird, 1992; Carsrud & Krueger, 1995; Katz & Gartner, 1988; Krueger & Brazeal, 1994).

The theoretical foundation of the research study is rooted in Ajzen's theory of planned behavior (see Figure 1) (Ajzen 1991; Ajzen & Fishbein, 1980). The theory of planned behavior suggests that behavior is predicted by behavioral intentions, which are a function of individual attitudes toward the behavior, a subjective norm, and perceived behavior control (Ajzen, 1991; Ajzen & Fishbein, 1980). Individual attitudes are a person's overall evaluation of whether performing the behavior is good or bad (Ajzen, 1991). A subjective norm is a person's belief that people who are important to the person think that he or she should, or should not, perform the behavior (Ajzen, 1991). Finally, perceived behavioral control is an individual's judgement of the likelihood of successfully performing the intended behavior (Ajzen, 1991).

Subsequent testing of the model has supported its validity by demonstrating the ability of intentions to predict behavior in a variety of situations (e.g., Ajzen, 1991; Doll & Ajzen, 1990; Nettemeyer, Andrews, & Durvasula, 1990; Schifter & Ajzen, 1985). In fact, research suggests that intentions are the single best predictor of planned behavior (Ajzen & Fishbein, 1980; Krueger et al., 1995). Entrepreneurship is clearly planned behavior (Krueger et al., 1995). Therefore, the formation of entrepreneurial intentions holds significant potential to predict entrepreneurial behavior.

Shapero (1982) extended the focus on intentions by developing an intentions-based model of the entrepreneurial event (see

**Figure 1. Ajzen's (1991) Theory of Planned Behavior**

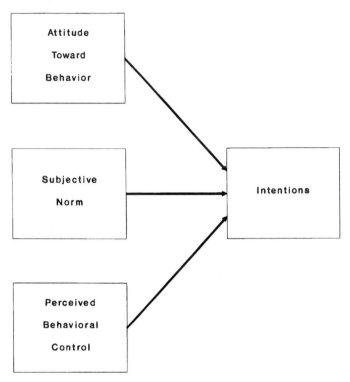

Figure 2). Like Ajzen, Shapero theorized that a person's intentions of starting a business would accurately predict his or her engaging in entrepreneurial activity (Shapero, 1982). He further suggested that the direct antecedents of entrepreneurial intentions consisted of the perceived desirability of starting a business, a person's perception of the feasibility of starting a business, and a person's propensity to take action (Krueger, 1993; Shapero, 1982). Shapero (1982) also suggested that the extent of past exposure to entrepreneurship (breadth) and an evaluation of the positiveness of the past experiences influence perceptions of desirability and feasibility (Krueger, 1993).

The perceived desirability of entrepreneurial activity is influenced by social forces, especially those forces of family and friends (e.g., Bird, 1988; Bygrave, 1997; Martin, 1984). Ajzen and Fishbein

**Figure 2. Shapero's (1982) Model of the Entrepreneurial Event**

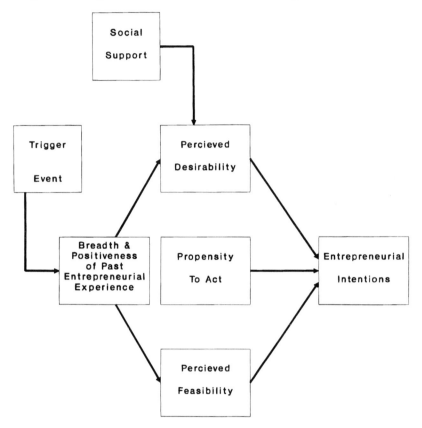

(1980) also provide support for this assertion by suggesting that the attitudes that help form intentions are influenced by what people (i.e., family, friends) who are important to the person forming the intentions think. Therefore, the literature suggests that the social influence of family and friends, or social support, impact the formation of entrepreneurial intentions.

Perceived feasibility is defined as ". . . the degree to which one believes that he or she is personally capable of starting a business" (Krueger, 1993 p. 8). Perceptions of feasibility appear closely related to the construct of perceived self-efficacy (Ajzen, 1991, 1987) as theorized in Bandura's social learning theory (Bandura,

1977). Self-efficacy is a comprehensive summary or judgement of a person's perceived capability of performing a specific task (Gist & Mitchell, 1992). Previous research has shown that self-efficacy predicts motivation and task performance in a variety of work-related situations (Gist, 1987) such as sales for insurance agents (Barling & Beattie, 1983), career choice (Lent, Brown, & Larkin, 1987), and adaptability to new technology (Hill, Smith, & Mann, 1987). Therefore, as suggested by Boyd and Vozikis (1994), self-efficacy is useful in explaining the process of evaluation and choice that surrounds the development of entrepreneurial intentions.

Gist and Mitchell (1992) suggested that perceptions of self-efficacy are determined by three types of assessments. First, there is an analysis of task requirements, which requires an individual to develop inferences about what it takes to perform the required task at various levels of performance. Second, individuals make an assessment of personal and situational resources and constraints. Third, individuals attribute past experiences of success or failure to the task to be performed (Gist & Mitchell, 1992).

Applying the three assessments to entrepreneurial behavior would suggest that individuals would first development inferences about what it takes to start a business such as opportunity recognition, writing a business plan, and obtaining financing. Next, the individual would assess his or her ability to perform the required tasks and the availability of the necessary resources to start a new business. Finally, the individual would draw on either positive or negative past entrepreneurial experience to help formulate his or her perceptions of the chances of successfully starting a new business.

Recognizing the importance of past experience, the Shapero (1982) model includes the influence of past entrepreneurial experience on the formation of perceived desirability and perceived feasibility (self-efficacy). The degree of influence is determined by both the amount of past entrepreneurial experience (breadth) and the positiveness of the experience (Krueger, 1993). For example, a person with extensive positive entrepreneurial experience will find starting a business more desirable and feasible than a person with limited positive experience. Consequently, a person with extensive negative past experience will find starting a business less desirable and feasible than a person with limited negative experience.

Shapero (1982) theorized that persons who find entrepreneurship desirable and feasible still may not form intentions because they lack, what he called, a propensity to act. He conceptualized propensity to act as being related to a person's perceptions of his or her ability to control and manipulate the environment. Locus of control was suggested as a proxy for the propensity to act construct (Shapero, 1982). Recent work by Bateman and Crant (1993), however, provides a more likely description of the construct conceptualized by Shapero. They identified what they describe as a proactive personality, which is expressed in what they term proactive behavior. Proactive behavior is behavior that alters environments (Bateman & Crant, 1993). This behavior is rooted in a person's need to control and manipulate the environment. Persons having a proactive personality tend to scan the environment for opportunities, show initiative, take action, and persevere until they reach closure and bring about change (Bateman & Crant, 1993). These are likely characteristics of a potential entrepreneur. In fact, the literature implies that a proactive personality is a significant predictor of entrepreneurial intentions (Crant, 1995).

Finally, Shapero (1982) as well as other researchers suggest that entrepreneurial activity is often triggered by some event such as loss of a job, birth of a child, marriage, and divorce (Baucus & Human, 1994; Bygrave, 1997; Holmes & Cartwright, 1993; Shapero, 1982). Additional support for the "trigger" concept comes from the related fields of career choice (Osipow & Fitzgerald, 1996) and organizational development (Gersick, 1991). Consequently, the literature suggests that the presence of a trigger event may enhance the formation of entrepreneurial intentions.

Although the models developed by Ajzen (1991) and Shapero (1982) are similar in their reasoning, research by Krueger et al., (1995) found that the Shapero model was a more robust predictor of entrepreneurial intentions. Therefore, the Shapero (1982) model may provide a stronger research foundation.

Based on this theoretical foundation, the following specific questions are addressed in the current research study:

1. How can intentions-based models such as the Ajzen (1991) and the Shapero (1982) models be combined to explain the formation of entrepreneurial intentions?

2. What important variables contribute to the formation of entrepreneurial intentions? Broadly speaking, how does one decide to become an entrepreneur?
3. Can the presence of a trigger event add anything to the understanding of the formation of entrepreneurial intentions?
4. How do situational variables such as past entrepreneurial experience, support from family and friends, and the availability of resources influence the formation of entrepreneurial intentions?

These research questions were explored in a field study with a sample of 125 junior college students in Texas. Fifty-six of the respondents consisted of students enrolled in one of the three real estate courses required for licensure (viz., real estate principles, real estate agency, or real estate law contracts), and 69 were enrolled in non-real estate courses designed for career development. Texas law requires that before individuals can become licensed to sell real estate, they must complete approved courses in Texas real estate principles, the law of agency, and law contracts. Therefore, of the students taking any of these courses, many will have the intention to start a real estate business while others, especially those in non-real estate courses, will not intend to start a real estate business. The sample used solves a weakness of previous entrepreneurial research in which samples of individuals who may not be involved in creating a new business were used (Gartner, 1989). At the same time, however, the inclusion in the sample of non-real estate students was necessary to ensure an adequate range in responses to questions that assess the significance of certain constructs in the formation of entrepreneurial intentions.

## SIGNIFICANCE OF RESEARCH

The research study was designed to answer the call of researchers for a better understanding of the birth of a new firm (e.g. Bull & Willard, 1993; Bygrave, 1989; Katz & Gartner, 1988; Low & MacMillian, 1988). Therefore, because of the potential predictive value of intentions-based models to explain entrepreneurial behavior (Ajzen, 1991; Ajzen & Fishbein, 1980; Bird, 1988; Krueger et al.,

1995) coupled with the lack of the empirical testing of such models (MacMillian & Katz, 1992; Krueger et al., 1995), the primary focus and significant contribution of the current study is the combining of several theoretical frameworks for the formation of entrepreneurial intentions into one parsimonious model.

The development of a conceptually sound, theory driven, and empirically tested intentions-based model provides several potential benefits. The research model contains both background and dispositional variables that combine to form the intentions to start a business. The model will help researchers understand how the background of the entrepreneur and the characteristics of the entrepreneur combine to form entrepreneurial intentions. This is important to researchers because it will provide a framework to help answer a variety of questions, such as "What impact does the development of a business plan have on the perceived desirability of starting a business?" or "How does teaching entrepreneurial skills impact entrepreneurial self-efficacy and ultimately entrepreneurial intentions?" (Krueger et al., 1995). In addition, understanding the influence of a trigger event would aid researchers in assessing how personal events such as marriage, divorce, and job loss influence the decision to start a new business.

For entrepreneurs and educators, knowing how entrepreneurial intentions are formed will yield a wealth of practical applications. For example, educators could develop entrepreneurial training that would increase the probability of intentions forming (Krueger et al., 1995). Entrepreneurs could understand how their intentions are formed and take steps to manipulate the critical variables such as to increase self-efficacy, increase desirability, and become more confident in their ability to take action.

Public policy makers will benefit from understanding the impact of policy initiatives that would encourage the formation of intentions and ultimately, the formation of new business. For example, the influence on entrepreneurial activity created by special economic incentives or the formation of incubator programs will be easier to assess. With the wave of corporate downsizing and outsourcing, community economic stability will hinge on new business formation (Krueger et al. 1995). Therefore, promoting entrepreneurial intentions is both desirable and feasible.

## DEFINITIONS OF TERMS

The following definitions are provided for key terms that are used throughout the study.

1. Entrepreneur/Entrepreneurship:
   The literature provides no universally accepted definition of an entrepreneur (Gartner, 1989). In fact, the subject has developed a great deal of controversy (Carland, Hoy, & Carland, 1988; Gartner, 1988). Therefore, as Gartner (1989) suggests, each research study should specifically define the type of entrepreneur that is the focus for that particular study. Consequently, the term entrepreneur is defined for this study as someone who starts an independent, profit-making business venture (Bird, 1989). Entrepreneurship is defined as the process of starting the business venture (Krueger, 1993).

2. Entrepreneurial Behavior:
   For this study, entrepreneurial behavior is defined as performing behavior that indicates a dedication to the physical creation of a business venture (Behave, 1994).

3. Entrepreneurial Intentions:
   Entrepreneurial intentions is defined for this study as the commitment to performing behavior that is necessary to physically start the business venture (Krueger, 1993; Krueger et al., 1995).

4. Trigger Event:
   Shapero (1975,1982) assumes that inertia guides human behavior until something interrupts or displaces that inertia (Krueger et al., 1995). Therefore, Shapero (1975) suggests that entrepreneurial activity is often triggered by a disrupting or displacing event. This event can be either positive (e.g., marriage) or negative (e.g., job loss). For this study, trigger event is defined as something (either positive or negative) that disrupts or displaces the inertia of human behavior.

5. Perceived Desirability:
   This study will use Shapero's definition of perceived desirability as described by Krueger (1993). It is defined ". . . as the degree to which one finds the prospect of starting a business to be attractive; in essence, it reflects one's affect toward entrepreneurship" (Krueger, 1993, p.8).

6. Propensity for Proactive Behavior:
   A person with a proactive personality is one who is relatively unconstrained by situational forces and who effects environmental change (Crant, 1996). The proactive personality identifies opportunities and acts on them; it shows initiative, takes action, and perseveres until it changes the environment (Crant, 1996). Therefore, propensity for proactive behavior is the tendency of individuals to act in a way consistent with a proactive personality.

7. Entrepreneurial Self-efficacy:
   Self-efficacy is a comprehensive summary or judgement of perceived capability of performing a specific task (Gist & Mitchell, 1992). Entrepreneurial self-efficacy is the degree to which one believes that he or she is capable of starting a business venture.

8. Entrepreneurial Self-efficacy Assessment:
   Gist and Mitchell (1992) suggest that self-efficacy judgements are partially determined by an assessment of task requirements, an assessment of one's ability to complete the task coupled with the availability of resources and the existence of constraints, and an assessment of past experiences. The assessment of past experience, however, is not as important as the other two assessments when the task is new to the individual (such as starting a new business) (Gist & Mitchell, 1992). Therefore, for this study, entrepreneurial self-efficacy assessment is defined as an individual assessment of what is takes to start a business venture coupled with perceived ability to complete the task and the availability of resources or the perceived lack of necessary resources.

9. Breadth and Positiveness of Past Entrepreneurial Experience:
   Shapero (1982) suggests that the quantity and quality of past entrepreneurial experience indirectly influences entrepreneurial intentions. Therefore, breadth of past entrepreneurial experience is defined as the extent to which a person has been exposed to entrepreneurship in the past. Positiveness is defined as whether the past experiences are perceived as positive or negative.

10. Social Support:
    Ajzen (1991) describes the construct of subjective norm as the social pressure to perform or not perform the intended

behavior. The social pressure is primarily determined by what important people (e.g., family, friends) in the life of the individual considering a particular behavior think about the performance of the behavior, and the strength of the individual's motive to comply with the wishes of the important others (Ajzen & Fishbein, 1980). As a result, social support is defined as perceptions of what important others think of an individual starting a business venture and the motivation of the individual to comply with the wishes of these others.

## CHAPTER SUMMARY

This chapter was designed to provide a broad overview of the research study. First, an introduction to the study was provided followed by a statement of the problem and the purpose of the study. The theoretical foundation including specific research questions to be addressed and the methodology to be used was presented for the study. Next, the significance of the research was presented followed by definitions of the relevant terms used throughout the study. Chapter II provides a review of the literature and development of the research model.

# Literature Review and Development of Research Model and Hypotheses

This chapter contains a review of the literature on the relationship between intentions and behavior, an introduction to intentions-based models of predicting behavior, and the theoretical development of the research model and related hypotheses. The first major section examines the ability of entrepreneurial intentions to predict entrepreneurial behavior. This section includes a discussion of the research that supports the ability of intentions to predict behavior, along with a description of assumptions and conditions necessary to ensure predictive ability. This discussion is followed by a section that applies the necessary assumptions and conditions to the entrepreneurial intentions-behavior relationship.

The second major section begins with a discussion of the literature that defines the nature of intentions and presents research support for the use of intentions-based models. The next two subsections introduce two of the primary intentions-based models that provide the theoretical framework for the study: Ajzen's (1991) theory of planned behavior and Shapero's (1982) model of the entrepreneurial event. Finally, the second major section concludes with a comparison of the theoretical foundation and predictive ability of the two models.

The third and final major section presents the entrepreneurial intentions-based research model and related hypotheses. This section presents an overview of the research model followed by four sections that discuss the major predictor variables of entrepreneurial intentions along with their antecedents and related hypotheses. The first of the four sections describes the theoretical foundation and related hypotheses associated with perceived desirability and its antecedents of social pressure, breadth of past entrepreneurial experience, and positiveness of past entrepreneurial experience. The second section presents propensity for proactive behavior along with its supporting research and related hypothesis. Next is a description of the supporting literature and theoretical development of entrepreneurial self-efficacy and its determinants of self-efficacy assessment, breadth of past entrepreneurial experience, and positiveness of past entrepreneurial experience along with appropriate hypotheses. Finally, the moderating effect of a trigger event on the relationship between perceived desirability, propensity for proactive behavior, and entrepreneurial self-efficacy and entrepreneurial intentions is described and supported with previous research.

## THE ABILITY OF ENTREPRENEURIAL INTENTIONS TO PREDICT ENTREPRENEURIAL BEHAVIOR

### The Intentions-Behavior Relationship

Whereas the primary purpose of the current study is to develop a model that links various variables to the formation of entrepreneurial intentions, the ultimate value of any intentions-based model of entrepreneurship is the prediction of entrepreneurial behavior based on measures of entrepreneurial intentions. Intentions are a reliable predictor of human behavior in a variety of situations, and are considered by many to be the most effective predictor of behavior (Ajzen, 1991; Ajzen & Fishbein, 1980; Krueger et al., 1995; Krueger, 1993). For example, intentions have been a significant predictor of job search activities (van Ryn & Vinokur, 1990), playing video games (Doll & Ajzen, 1990), performance on cognitive tasks (Locke, Bobko, & Lee, 1984), election participation (Watters, 1989), and gift giving (Netemeyer, Andrews, & Durvasula, 1990).

Intentions are assumed to capture the motivational factors that influence behavior. They are indications of how hard people are willing to work and how much effort they will expend to perform the intended behavior. As a general rule, the stronger the intentions, the more likely they are to predict the intended behavior (Ajzen, 1991).

The predictive value of intentions rests, however, on several assumptions and conditions (Ajzen, 1991; Ajzen & Fishbein, 1980). First, behavior must be planned and under the volitional control of the individual; not uncontrolled and spontaneous. Second, people must feel that their chances of success are good. Third, there must be a correspondence between the measures of behavior and the elements of intentions-action, target, context, and time. Finally, the predictive value of intentions is influenced by the stability of intentions between the time intentions are measured and the time the corresponding behaviors are measured. When these assumptions and conditions are satisfied, correspondence exists between measures of behavior and the elements of intentions, and when intentions remain stable during the measurement process, the predictive value of intentions is greatly enhanced (Ajzen & Fishbein, 1980).

The assumption that behavior must be planned and under volitional control for it to be predicted by intentions was imposed by Ajzen and Fishbein (1980). Behavioral intentions can be expressed only in behavior that a person can decide to perform or not perform at will (volitional control) (Ajzen, 1991, 1985). As a general rule, humans are usually rational in their behavior. Important social behavior is not uncontrolled and spontaneous, but is thought about and planned. Individuals consider the implications of their behavior before they engage in the behavior (Ajzen, 1991). If a person's actions are under volitional control and are thought about in advance, then a person's intention to take action is a direct determinant of behavior (Ajzen & Fishbein, 1980). Conversely, behavior not planned or under volitional control will not necessarily be directly determined by intentions.

Behavior also may depend on non-motivational factors such as availability of opportunity or necessary resources (e.g., time, money, skill) (Ajzen, 1985). The availability of an opportunity and necessary resources will, to some extent, determine the likelihood of behavioral action. A person who has the opportunity and resources necessary to take action is said to have actual behavioral control of the intended behavior. From a psychological stand point, however, it is not the actual availability of resources and opportunity, but perception of behavioral control that influences behavior. Therefore, the capability of intentions to predict behavior is influenced by the degree of a person's perceived behavioral control (Ajzen, 1991). ". . . Perceived behavioral control refers to people's perception of the ease or difficulty of performing the behavior of interest" (Ajzen, 1991, p. 183).

Unlike Rotter's (1966) locus of control, which posits that outcomes are a result of individual action, perceived behavioral control is a judgement of a person's chances of successfully completing the behavior, much like Bandura's (1977, 1982) construct of self-efficacy (Ajzen, 1991). For example, a person may feel that becoming a surgeon is a result of individual action (locus of control), but his or her chances of successfully becoming one are slim (perceived behavioral control) because of a lack of opportunity or necessary resources. Carrying the reasoning further, a person may have the intention to execute a certain behavior (e.g., start a business), but perceives that the chances of success are poor. Therefore, intentions will be less likely to predict behavior because of a perception of little or no behavioral control. The greater the perception of behavioral control, the better intentions will predict behavior (Ajzen, 1991).

For intentions to accurately predict behavior, there also must be a correspondence between the measure of behavior and the action, target (Kim & Hunter, 1993), context, and time elements of the intention measure (Ajzen & Fishbein, 1980; Sheppard, Hartwick, & Warshaw, 1988). For a single-action behavior, there must be a target of the action, a context in which the action takes place, and a time element. For example, "I intend to seek (action) employment (target) at XYZ Corporation (context) next week (time)" is a statement of intended behavior to seek employment in a specific context during a specific time. The measure of behavior must correspond to the action, target, context, and time elements of intention by asking if the subject sought employment at XYZ Corporation during the next week. The ability of intentions to predict behavior would be weakened if the behavior measurement had asked only if the subject had sought employment while ignoring the time and context elements. The closer the correspondence of the measures of intention and behavior, the better intentions predict behavior (Ajzen & Fishbein, 1980).

Finally, intentions must remain stable between the time the intentions are measured and the time the corresponding behavior is measured (Ajzen & Fishbein, 1980). Unexpected events, changes in attitude, and changes in perception of behavioral control could destabilize intentions. Generally, the shorter the time between measurement of intentions and the corresponding behavior, the greater the predictive ability of intentions (Ajzen & Fishbein, 1980).

In summary, intentions have been shown to be good predictors of behavior if the basic assumptions and conditions are satisfied. First, behavior must be planned and under the volitional control of the individual. Second, an individual's perceived behavioral control must be relatively high. Third, there must be a correspondence between measures of intention and behavior among the elements of action, target, context, and time. Finally, the time between the formation of intentions and the behavior must be short enough to allow intentions to remain stable. Table 1 provides a summary of the research investigating the ability of intentions to predict behavior.

## Application of the Assumptions and Conditions Necessary to Ensure the Predictive Value of the Intentions-Behavior Relationship to Entrepreneurial Intentions-Behavior

Although the research study concentrates on the formation of entrepreneurial intentions, the value of the study will be enhanced if entrepreneurial intentions are able to predict entrepreneurial behavior. To ensure that an intentions-based model of entrepreneurship will be able to predict entrepreneurial behavior, the four

**Table 1. The Ability of Intentions to Predict Behavior**

| Study | Behavior | Support |
|---|---|---|
| van Ryn & Vinokur (1990) | Job Search | Yes |
| Doll & Ajzen (1990) | Playing six video games | Yes |
| Schlegel et al., (1990) | Problem Drinking | Yes |
| Locke et al., (1984) | Performance on cognitive tasks | Yes |
| Schifter & Ajzen (1985) | Losing Weight | Yes |
| Netemeyer, Andrews, & Durvasula (1990) | Gift giving | Yes |

assumptions and conditions introduced in the previous section must apply to the entrepreneurial intention-behavior relationship. First, entrepreneurial behavior must be under the volitional control of the individual. Second, the individual must feel that his or her chances of starting a business are good. Third, there must be a correspondence between the measures of intentions and behavior. Finally, measures of intentions must remain stable between the time the measure of intentions is made and the time the measure of behavior is made.

Learned's (1992) model of the start-up (founding) of a new venture provides a convenient framework for discussing the application of the four basic assumptions and conditions necessary to ensure the predictive value of the entrepreneurial intention-behavior relationship. Learned suggested that the founding process has four basic dimensions which proceed in the following order: 1) propensity to found, 2) intention to found (entrepreneurial intention), 3) sense making, and 4) the decision to found (entrepreneurial behavior). Some individuals have a combination of psychological traits (i.e., locus of control, need for achievement) that interact with background factors (i.e., family, education, experience) to give them a propensity to found. When these individuals encounter situations (i.e., opportunity, pull of a mentor) that combine with their background and traits, they form intentions. People with entrepreneurial intentions interact with the environment while they gather resources to make the new venture a reality. As a result, individuals make the decision to start, or abandon the attempt to start, a business based upon the sense made of the attempt (Learned, 1992).

The first assumption (Ajzen & Fishbein, 1980) suggests that entrepreneurial behavior must be under the volitional control of the individual. As described by Learned's (1992) framework, entrepreneurial organizations emerge over time as a result of careful thought and action. Therefore, entrepreneurial behavior is an example of planned behavior under the volitional control of the entrepreneur (e.g., Behave, 1994; Bird, 1988; Katz & Gartner, 1988). Starting a business is not done with unconscious motives or overpowering desires coupled with thoughtless behavior.

The second assumption (Ajzen & Fishbein, 1980) indicates that the individual must feel that his or her chances of successful entrepreneurship are good. Perceptions of chances for success would form during the propensity to found and the intentions to found stages of Learned's (1992) framework. Perceptions of success are captured in Ajzen's (1991, 1985) concept of perceived behavioral control. Perceived behavioral control is a measure of a person's perceived likelihood of behavioral achievement (Ajzen, 1991). Ajzen (1991) suggests that the higher the perceptions of behavioral control, the stronger the intentions-behavior relationship. Therefore, for any intentions-based model of entrepreneurship to be successful at predicting entrepreneurial behavior, the entrepreneur needs to have a fairly high perception of behavioral control (i.e., perceptions that the chances of success are good).

The third condition (Ajzen & Fishbein, 1980) is the need for correspondence between the measure of entrepreneurial intention and the measure of entrepreneurial behavior as to action, target, context, and time. The degree of correspondence between the measure of intention and behavior poses potential problems for the entrepreneurial intention-behavior relationship. Prior research has tended to measure intention with a broad-scoped question such as, "Do you think you will ever start a business?" (e.g., Crant, 1996; Krueger et al., 1995; Krueger, 1993). The corresponding measure of behavior that includes "will ever" (time), "start" (action), and "a business" (target) raises some questions and issues. For example, "will ever" is an indefinite time period, at what point the business is to "start" has not been defined, what "a business" is has not been determined, and what kind of business (context) have been ignored. As Ajzen and Fishbein (1980) state, the greater the correspondence between the intention elements of action, target, time, and context and the measure of behavior, the better the predictive ability of the intentions-behavior relationship. Therefore, to enhance predictive ability, any measure of intentions to start a business must correspond to the intended behavior.

Correspondence can be improved by simply stating a definite time period, a specific kind of business, and defining "business" as an independent profit-making venture (Ajzen & Fishbein, 1980; Bird, 1989). The action element "start" poses the most serious problem. Behave (1994) suggested that the entrepreneur's commitment to physical creation is a critical transition point in the development of a business. This is the point at which the entrepreneur realizes that internal effort and resources are not sufficient to get the business going and that he or she must seek outside help and make a commitment to take physical action to create the firm. This would describe the end of the two dimensions of propensity to found and intention to found, and the beginning of the two dimensions of sense making and decision to found (Learned, 1992).

Research suggests several potential activities that would indicate a commitment to physical creation such as securing a location, purchasing supplies, hiring employees, leasing equipment, and applying for financing (Gatewood, Shaver, & Gartner, 1995; Vesper, 1990). Using activities that indicate a commitment to physical creation as the action element of intentions could improve the predictive ability of the intention-behavior relationship. For example, "Do you think you will apply for bank financing in the next six months to start a clothing store?" would more accurately describe the action, target, context, and time elements of intention rather than "Do you think you will ever start a business?" The corresponding behavior measure would simply ask "Did you apply for bank financing to start a clothing store during the past six months?"

The lack of correspondence is a potential weakness of past entrepreneurial research (Gartner, 1989). For example, much of the previous entrepreneurial intention-behavior research has been conducted on students who may not know what activities are required to start a business, what type of business they want to start, or the time frame for starting the venture (e.g., Crant, 1996; Krueger et al., 1995; Krueger, 1993). In this case, it would be difficult to specifically describe the action, target, time, and context in the measure of intention. The lack of specific correspondence could weaken the predictive ability of the intention-behavior relationship (Ajzen & Fishbein, 1980).

Finally, entrepreneurial intentions need to remain stable between the time of the measure of intentions and the measure of entrepreneurial behavior. As the entrepreneur interacts with the environment while he or she gathers resources and information (the sense making dimension) (Learned, 1992), a variety of factors (e.g., the economy, family support, entrepreneurial self-efficacy) may change and destabilize intentions. Therefore, the measurement of entrepreneurial intentions and behavior should be made as close together as possible (Ajzen & Fishbein, 1980).

From the preceding discussion, the following conclusion can be drawn. In the context of entrepreneurial behavior as planned and under the volitional control of the entrepreneur, the ability of entrepreneurial intentions to predict such behavior has the potential to be very strong if the following conditions are met. The entrepreneur must have a fairly high degree of perceived behavioral control. Measures of entrepreneurial intentions must correspond to measures of behavior in action, target, time, and context. Measurements of the intention-behavior relationship need to be made in a short enough time frame for intentions to remain stable.

## THE NATURE OF INTENTIONS AND INTRODUCTION OF INTENTIONS-BASED MODELS OF ENTREPRENEURIAL BEHAVIOR

New business ventures do not "just happen." They are developed through the vision, goals, and motivation of individuals. New businesses are the direct outcome of the entrepreneur's intentions and consequent actions, as moderated or influenced by environmental conditions (Bird, 1992). Because new ventures are the result of the individual and his or her actions, research on entrepreneurship has concentrated on the individual and his or her traits (Carland, Hoy, & Carland, 1988) and the actions of the individual (Gartner, 1985). The link between the individual and his or her actions is captured in the construct of intentions, which takes into account the impact of factors such as attitudes (Ajzen & Fishbein, 1980), social pressure (Ajzen & Fishbein, 1980; Shapero & Sokol 1982), past experience (Bird, 1988; Krueger, 1993; Shapero & Sokol, 1982), and individual personality (Bird, 1988, Shapero & Sokol, 1982). The planned behavior of starting a business is best predicted directly by intentions and not by attitudes, beliefs, personality, or demographics (Krueger et al., 1995).

Intention is a state of mind that directs a person's attention, experience, and behavior toward a specific objective or method of behaving (Bird, 1992). Intentions act as a perceptual filter for understanding the complex relationships, resources, and exchanges necessary for venture creation. Intentions direct action in alignment with the entrepreneur's goal of starting a business (Bird, 1992). Therefore, Krueger (1993) argues that intentions are the underpinnings of new organizations. Extending Krueger's argument further leads to the conclusion that intentions-based models of entrepreneurial behavior provide a coherent, parsimonious, highly generalized, and robust way of explaining and predicting such behavior (Katz & Gartner, 1988; Krueger et al., 1995; Shaver & Scott, 1992).

Intentions-based models provide the foundation for much of the empirical and conceptual entrepreneurial research (see Table 2). This is the result of earlier empirical research that has shown a weak predictive relationship between attitudes and behavior, and between a variety of exogenous variables such as personality traits, demographics, environmental factors, and employment status and behavior (Krueger et al., 1995). Ajzen (1991, 1985) proposed that attitudes do not work directly on behavior, but indirectly through intentions. In addition, attitudes are influenced by many exogenous variables, which also act indirectly on behavior through the intention-behavior relationship. As a result, the real power of intentions-based models of entrepreneurship is their ability to capture entrepreneurial attitudes as well as the effect of

**Table 2. Summary of Entrepreneurship Research
with Intentions as a Primary Focus**

| Author (s) | Research Foundation | Empirical | Conceptual |
|---|---|---|---|
| Bird (1988) | A | | X |
| Bird (1992) | A | | X |
| Bird & Jelinek (1988) | A | | X |
| Boyd & Vozikis (1994) | A | | X |
| Brenner, Pringel, & Greenhaus (1991) | A | X | |
| Crant (1996) | A | X | |
| Gartner (1988) | N | | X |
| Katz & Gartner (1988) | N | | X |
| Krueger (1993) | S | X | |
| Krueger & Brazeal (1994) | S | | X |
| Krueger, Reilly, & Carsrud (1995) | S & A | X | |
| Learned (1992) | N | | X |

A = Ajzen's (Theory of Planned Behavior)
S = Shapero's (Model of the Entrepreneurial Event)
N = Models other than Ajzen or Shapero

exogenous variables on attitudes in one theory-driven framework. This supports the call to develop more process models of entrepreneurial cognition that focus on intentions and their development (Katz & Gartner, 1988; Shaver & Scott, 1992).

With the exception of Learned (1992), this intentions focused research investigates the antecedents of intentions and the process of how intentions are formed. Learned's work uses intentions to help explain the process of new venture creation. Ajzen's theory of planned behavior (Ajzen, 1991, 1985; Ajzen & Fishbein, 1980) and Shapero's model of the entrepreneurial event (Shapero, 1982; Shapero & Sokol, 1982) have provided the theoretical foundation for most of this stream of research. The following section details both models.

## Ajzen's Theory of Planned Behavior

Intentions are formed by three primary attitudinal determinants; attitude toward the behavior, subjective (social) norm, and perceived behavioral control (see Figure 1 in Chapter 1; Ajzen, 1991). Attitude toward the behavior is simply a person's judgment that performing the intended behavior is good or bad and that he or she is in favor of, or against, the behavior. As a general rule, a person who believes that performing a behavior will lead to positive results will hold a positive attitude toward the behavior, while a person who believes the outcome will be negative will hold an unfavorable attitude toward the behavior. The theory of planned behavior holds that attitudes act through intentions to influence behavior.

Early scholars argued that attitudes could explain human behavior directly (e.g., Krech, Crutchfield, & Ballachey, 1962). This argument persisted until the 1930s when evidence began to emerge suggesting that attitudes could not directly predict behavior. LePiere (1934) found in a survey of 128 restaurants, hotels, and other establishments that over 90% of the respondents stated they would not accept members of the Chinese race in their establishments. When the same Chinese couple appeared at each of these establishments, however, they were refused service only twice. This raised serious questions concerning the attitude-behavior link. The attitude toward the Chinese race did not predict behavior toward the Chinese couple. Evidence continued to mount that attitudes were not always a direct predictor of behavior (Ajzen & Fishbein, 1980). In a review of the literature, Wicker (1969) found almost no relation between attitudes and behavior.

To solve the attitude-behavior discrepancies, Rosenberg and Hovaland (1960) suggested that attitudes are a multidimensional complex system consisting of a person's affect (feelings) towards an object, cognitive beliefs about the object, and his or her behavior toward the object. Therefore, when attitudes are studied from the perspective of affect, cognitive beliefs, and behavior, more significant relationships are found (e.g., Breckler, 1984). Ajzen and Fishbein (1980) argue, however, that in spite of the multidimensional approach, support for a direct attitude-behavior relationship remains weak.

Finally, some researchers have taken an "other variables approach," which assumes that attitudes are only one of a number of factors that impact behavior (Ajzen & Fishbein, 1980). Among other variables that have been suggested to impact behavior are conflicting attitudes; competing motives; verbal, intellectual, and social abilities; individual differences, such as personality characteristics; normative prescriptions of proper behavior; and expected or actual consequences of the behavior (Ajzen & Fishbein, 1980). There are so many potential variables, that even if some are significant predictors of behavior, they do not add to the understanding of the attitude-behavior relationship because no single variable can explain enough of the variance to be helpful (Schuman & Johnson, 1976).

Ajzen and Fishbein's (1980) solution to the problem is to restrict attitudes to a person's overall evaluation of whether performing the behavior is good or bad (affect component), and to clearly separate attitudes, intentions, and behavior with attitudes influencing behavior through intentions. In addition, Ajzen (1991) suggests that intentions are a better predictor of behavior than attitudes because intentions are determined by more than just attitudes. They also capture a judgement of what important other people think of the intended behavior (subjective norm) and a person's perception of the likelihood of successfully completing the behavior (perceived behavioral control).

In Ajzen's (1991) model, a subjective norm is the belief that people who are important to the individual think he or she should, or should not, perform the intended behavior. These beliefs are also influenced by the person's motivation to comply with the people who are most important to him or her. For example, a person considering starting a business may consider what his or her spouse thinks of the idea to start the business and how much the person wants to do what the spouse desires. The spouse may not like the idea to start the business, but if the individual is not motivated to do what the spouse wants, he or she may start the business anyway. Normally, if a person believes that most significant referents think the behavior should be performed, he or she will perceive social pressure to perform the behavior. Conversely, if a person believes that most significant referents are against the behavior, he or she will feel social pressure to avoid the behavior.

Finally, intentions are determined by a person's perceptions of behavioral control. Perceived behavioral control is an individual's judgement of the likelihood of performing the intended behavior successfully. The person judges the viability of the opportunity, the availability of resources, and his or her ability to perform the required tasks. This is most akin to Bandura's (1977, 1982) concept of self-efficacy, which is a judgement of how well one can execute the courses of action required to deal with prospective situations. Overall, the greater the perceptions of behavioral control, the greater the intentions of performing the desired behavior. Perceived behavioral control may not be particularly useful, however, if perceptions are unrealistic because the individual has little information about the behavior, the requirements or availability of resources have changed, or unfamiliar conditions enter the situation.

Meta-analyses of empirical tests of the Ajzen model applied in a variety of situations indicate that attitudes and perceived behavioral control, on average, explain over 50% of the variance in intentions and intentions explain over 30% of the variance in behavior (Sheppard, Hartwick, & Warshaw, 1988; Kim & Hunter, 1993). The explanation of 30% of the variance in behavior by intentions is considered a good improvement over the typical 10% explained by trait measures or by attitudes acting directly on behavior (Ajzen, 1991). In a review of several empirical tests of the subjective norm construct, Ajzen (1991) found mixed results and no clear link was established. Table 3 provides examples of empirical tests of the Ajzen (1991) model. Overall, the results provide support for part of Ajzen's intentions-based model.

*The Formation of Entrepreneurial Intentions*

**Table 3. Research Using the Ajzen (1991) Model**

| Study | Intention | Support for AB | SN | PBC |
|-------|-----------|:--------------:|:--:|:---:|
| van Ryn & Vinokur (1990) | Search for a job | Yes | Yes | Yes |
| Watters (1989) | Election participation | Yes | No | Yes |
| | Voting choice | Yes | No | Yes |
| Netemeyer, Burton & Johnston (1990) | Lose weight | Yes | No | Yes |
| Beal & Manstead (1991) | Limit infant's sugar intake | Yes | No | Yes |
| Parker et al., (1990) | Commit traffic violations | Yes | Yes | Yes |
| Godin et al., (1990) | Exercise after coronary | Yes | No | Yes |

AB = Attitude toward the behavior
SN = Subjective norm
PCB = Perceive behavioral control

## Shapero's Model of the Entrepreneurial Event

Underlying Shapero's (1982) model of the entrepreneurial event (see Figure 2 in Chapter 1), is the assumption that most individuals are held on a given life path by the inertia of their daily lives (Shapero & Sokol, 1982) until a major displacement disrupts the inertia. People are more likely to act based on negative displacements (e.g., loss of job, job dissatisfaction, divorce). At times, however, positive displacements (e.g., support of a partner, support from a mentor, support from a customer) can initiate action. Once the disruption of inertia occurs, the choice of action depends on the perceived desirability and feasibility of the action coupled with an individual's propensity to take action. Therefore, entrepreneurial intentions that lead to the entrepreneurial event have three primary determinants: perceived desirability, perceived feasibility, and a propensity to take action.

Perception of desirability is the degree to which one finds start-ing a business an attractive thing to do (Shapero, 1982). Perception of feasibility is the degree to which one thinks that he or she is capa-ble of starting a business. Similar to perceptions of behavioral control in Ajzen's (1991) model, perceived feasibility is much like Bandura's self-efficacy (Krueger, 1993). One must believe that starting a busi-ness is both desirable and feasible before entrepreneurial intentions are formed.

In the Shapero (1982) model, social pressure (what impor-tant others think of the behavior) influences intentions through perceived desirability. Shapero theorized that social pressure from important others such as family, friends, peer groups, and mentors influenced the formation of perceived desirability which in turn helps to determine entrepreneurial intentions (Shapero & Sokol, 1982). For example, social pressure from important others that places a high value on innovation and entrepreneurship will tend to encourage individuals to form favorable perceptions of desirability. Consequently, social pres-sure opposed to entrepreneurship will create unfavorable per-ceptions of desirability. Shapero's (1982) idea has empirical sup-port from studies by Krueger (1993) and Scherer et al., (1989) who found that the impact of role models (a form of social support) on the formation of intentions was worked indirectly through their impact on attitudes such as perceived desirability. As a result, in the Shapero (1982) model, social support is not a direct influence on the formation of intentions, but works through perceptions of desirability.

In addition, Shapero (1982) suggested that the extent (breadth) and positiveness of past entrepreneurial experiences are two other important factors in determining perceptions of desirability and feasibility. Individuals with a great deal of past entrepreneurial experience, especially if it was positive, will be more likely to form favorable perceptions of desirability and feasibility about entre-preneurial activity. Krueger (1993) found empirical support for the influence of breadth and positiveness of past experience on the perceptions of desirability and feasibility.

Shapero (1982) also theorized that the formation of entrepre-neurial intentions is determined by a person's propensity to act. Propensity to act is a disposition to act on one's decisions and is a result of one's desire to take control through taking action (Krueger,

1993). In general, the higher the propensity to act, the more likely a person is to take action on an intention.

The Shapero (1982) model has not received much research attention. Recent empirical tests, however, have shown significant support for Shapero's model (Krueger et al., 1995; Krueger, 1993). These studies provide the primary support for the model and show that perceptions of desirability, feasibility, and a propensity to act are all positively related to entrepreneurial intentions.

## A Comparison of the Ajzen and Shapero Models

The two models are more similar than they are different. Each model has a measure of attitude [attitude toward the behavior-Ajzen (1991); perceived desirability-Shapero (1982)] and a measure akin to Bandura's self-efficacy [perceived behavioral control-Ajzen (1991); perceived feasibility-Shapero (1982)]. Unlike Ajzen, Shapero suggests that social pressure, or subjective norm in the Ajzen (1991) model, influences intentions indirectly through perceived desirability (Krueger, 1993) and not directly as Ajzen proposes.

In addition, Shapero's model includes propensity to act as an influence on intentions, whereas Ajzen's model does not. Shapero (1982) reasoned that having positive perceptions of feasibility and desirability are not enough for firm creation, and that people also need a disposition to take action on their positive attitudes. Recent research by Reynolds (1992) provides support by suggesting that many individuals who have favorable attitudes towards entrepreneurship may never complete the formation of a new business, implying that a good attitude is not enough. A volitional aspect of "propensity to act" may be required. Shapero's (1982) conceptualization posits that propensity to act depends on one's desire to take control by taking action. A person is unlikely to have serious intentions toward entrepreneurial behavior without perceiving a likelihood of taking action to perform the behavior (Krueger, 1993).

Finally, the Shapero (1982) model assumes that some type of displacing event may be necessary to stimulate the process. After reviewing several studies examining the formation of new businesses, Shapero (1975) noticed that in most of the cases of new business formation, a displacing event triggered the business formation process. As a result, the Shapero (1982) model includes environmental displacements (i.e., trigger events) as necessary to start the entrepreneurial process. The Ajzen (1991) model does not include a trigger event, which implies that the trigger event may be unique to entrepreneurship. This is one of the areas of investigation in the current study.

Krueger and his associates (1995) conducted an empirical comparison of the two models and their ability to predict entrepreneurial intentions. Results provided support for both models. The test of the Ajzen (1991) model supported the predictive ability of attitude toward the behavior and perceptions of behavioral control (self-efficacy) to predict intentions. Social (subjective) norms, however, were not significant in the regression equation for the Ajzen (1991) model. On the other hand, the test of the Shapero (1982) model indicated strong support for perceived feasibility (self-efficacy), perceived desirability, and propensity to act. One potential problem with the test of the Shapero model is the omission of an environmental displacement from the test. Overall, however, the Shapero model appears to be a stronger framework for assessing entrepreneurial intentions.

## DEVELOPMENT OF RESEARCH MODEL AND HYPOTHESES

As previously discussed, research suggests that intentions are a reliable predictor of behavior if the four basic assumptions and conditions have been satisfied (Ajzen & Fishbein, 1980). As a result, the predictive value of the intentions-behavior relationship is well established in the literature. Therefore, the research model focuses on the variables that may relate to the formation of entrepreneurial intentions rather than on the intentions-behavior relationship.

Based on strong empirical support (e.g., Ajzen, 1991; Krueger, 1993; Krueger et al., 1995), the Ajzen (1991) and Shapero (1982) models, taken together, provide a solid foundation for research on influences on the formation of entrepreneurial intentions. The findings of Krueger et al., (1995), however, indicate that the Shapero model may be the better predictor of intentions. Therefore, the Shapero model is the primary foundation of the research model; although, as indicated earlier, the Ajzen model incorporates similar variables and, thus, lends itself well to the theoretical framework. Figure 3 presents the research model used in this study.

## Figure 3. Research Model of Entrepreneurial Intentions

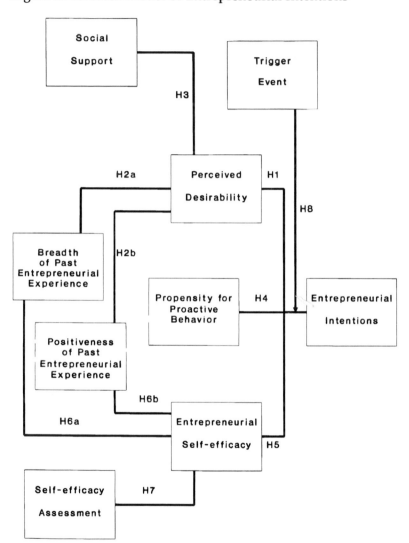

The construct of intentions has been previously discussed. For clarification purposes, however, entrepreneurial intentions will be defined in the context of the research model. Intention was described as a state of mind that directs a person's attention, experience, and behavior toward a specific object or method of behaving (Bird, 1992). This implies that intention directs individuals towards a specific action (behavior). A person with intentions has a commitment to a particular behavior. In fact, Krueger (1993) defined entrepreneurial intentions as the commitment to starting a business venture. In addition, intentions have the elements of action, target, time, and context. The critical elements are action and target. For this study, the target of entrepreneurial intentions is starting a profit-making enterprise, and the action is a behavior that is critical to making the enterprise a physical reality (i.e., securing a location, purchasing supplies, hiring employees). Therefore, in the research model, entrepreneurial intention is the commitment to the physical creation of a profit making business.

Overall, the research model suggests that entrepreneurial intentions are formed by three primary factors: perceived desirability, propensity for proactive behavior, and entrepreneurial self-efficacy. The basic premise of the model is that entrepreneurial intentions are formed when people perceive that entrepreneurship is desirable, they believe that they are capable of doing what is required, and they take action on their beliefs.

Perceived desirability is Shapero's (1982) construct defined as the degree to which one finds the prospect of starting a business attractive. This is similar to attitude toward the behavior in Ajzen's (1991) model. In addition, perceived desirability is influenced by social support (what important others think) and the breadth (quantity) and positiveness (quality) of past entrepreneurial experience (Shapero, 1982; Krueger, 1993).

Shapero (1982) theorized that positive attitudes alone were not enough to produce entrepreneurial intentions, but also required a propensity to take action. Shapero posited that propensity to take action is rooted in a person's desire to take control. He proposed locus of control as a proxy variable (Krueger, 1993). Locus of control, however, often fails to separate entrepreneurs from managers (Brockhaus & Horwitz, 1986). Propensity for proactive behavior, however, is a new construct that may provide a better measure of what Shapero had in mind.

Propensity for proactive behavior is a personality type that is relatively unconstrained by situational forces, identifies opportunities, and acts on them (Bateman & Crant, 1993). It is a result of one's need to manipulate and control the situation (Langer, 1983). This construct captures the idea of control, which is the central theme of Shapero's (1982) propensity to act. As a result, propensity for proactive behavior is included in the research model as necessary for the formation of entrepreneurial intentions.

Entrepreneurial self-efficacy is a summary judgement of one's capability of starting a business. It is the degree to which one believes that he or she is capable of starting a new venture. This construct is similar to perceived feasibility in Shapero's (1992) model and perceived behavioral control in Ajzen's (1991) model, but captures more of the cognitive assessments an individual makes about required skills, resources, environmental conditions, and implications of past experience (Gist & Mitchell, 1992). Because self-efficacy is influenced by past experience (Gist & Mitchell, 1992), the model suggests that entrepreneurial self-efficacy is influenced by both the breadth (quantity) and positiveness (quality) of past entrepreneurial experience (Krueger, 1993). In addition, entrepreneurial self-efficacy is influenced by a self-efficacy assessment (Gist & Mitchell, 1992). The self-efficacy assessment is an assessment of what it takes to start a business in terms of the perceived availability of necessary skills, ability, and resources (Gist & Mitchell, 1992).

Finally, as theorized by Shapero and Sokol (1982), individuals live in a state of inertia until some disrupting event takes place. This trigger event is more likely to be negative (e.g., job loss) than positive (e.g., birth of a child). Once the trigger event happens, the intention toward action depends on perceived desirability and perceived self-efficacy of the action combined with a proactive personality to take the action. Recent research by Gersick (1991) suggests, however, that whereas change can be gradual in some situations, a trigger event can often enhance and stimulate the change process in other situations. For example, an individual may gradually develop the intention to become an entrepreneur because of the perceived desirability of doing so, the individual's belief in his or her ability to do so, and his or her propensity to take action. This process may evolve over time as information is obtained concerning the individual's ability and the prospect of successfully becoming an entrepreneur. On the other hand, the individual's intentions may be "hurried along" by a trigger event. Theoretically, this suggests the presence of a trigger event as a moderator of the relationship between the three primary determinants and entrepreneurial intentions. That is, a trigger event will enhance the relationship, but is not absolutely necessary for the formation of entrepreneurial intentions.

This section has provided an overview of the study's research model. The following sections will more fully develop the theoretical foundation for each variable and describe the associated hypotheses.

## Perceived Desirability and Entrepreneurial Intentions

Both the Ajzen (1991) and the Shapero (1982) models include similar measures of attitude as a determinant of intentions. In each case, attitude is an evaluative measure of the desirability of performing the intended behavior. Thus, in the research model used in the study, perceived desirability is a measure of a person's attitude toward starting a business. It is important to note that attitudes (perceived desirability) include evaluations of actions not objects. For example, a person's attitude toward women may not impact his or her action concerning women. A person may not like women (object) but hire (action) them anyway. Only a person's specific attitude toward hiring women would predict whether or not he or she will hire them (Ajzen & Fishbein, 1980). Therefore, perceived desirability is an evaluation of starting a business (entrepreneurship), not an evaluation of entrepreneurs.

Empirical support for the attitude-intentions relationship is strong. A recent meta-analysis of empirical studies of the attitude-intentions association indicated that over 50% of the variance in intentions is explained by attitudes toward the behavior (Kim & Hunter, 1993; Sheppard et al., 1988). Table 4 provides an overview of the empirical support for the relationship between the attitude toward the behavior (Ajzen, 1991) and intentions, and perceived desirability (Shapero, 1982) and intentions.

Attitudes about any behavior (in this case, starting a business) are determined by the individual's beliefs about performing the behavior (Ajzen & Fishbein, 1980). Beliefs are formed by associating the intended behavior with various characteristics, qualities,

**Table 4. Research in which the Attitude-Intentions Link
          is Examined**

| Study | Intentions | Construct | Support |
|-------|-----------|-----------|---------|
| Doll & Ajzen (1990) | Play six video game | AB | Yes |
| Watters (1989) | Participate in elections and voting choice | AB | Yes |
| Schifter & Ajzen (1985) | Lose weight | AB | Yes |
| Parker et al., (1990) | Commit traffic violations | AB | Yes |
| Godin et al., (1990) | Exercise after coronary | AB | Yes |
| Krueger (1993) | Entrepreneurial | PD | Yes |
| Krueger et al., (1995) | Entrepreneurial | PD & AB | Yes |

AB = Attitude Toward the Behavior
PD = Perceived Desirability

and attributes. From these associations, individuals will either like (have a favorable attitude) or dislike (have an unfavorable attitude) toward performing the behavior (Ajzen & Fishbein, 1980). Individuals with favorable attitudes toward a behavior will be more likely to form strong entrepreneurial intentions and, thus, perform the behavior than individuals with unfavorable attitudes (Ajzen & Fishbein, 1980). As a result, the following hypothesis is suggested.

H1.  Perceived desirability is positively associated with the formation of entrepreneurial intentions.

People develop beliefs during the normal course of their lives. These beliefs may be the result of direct involvement and/or observation, or the acceptance of information from outside sources (verbal persuasion) (Ajzen & Fishbein, 1980). Therefore, the research model suggests that two major sources of beliefs influence the formation of perceived desirability. First, the breadth and positiveness of past experiences, which are evaluations of the quantity and quality of past entrepreneurial experience, provide information concerning the desirability of entrepreneurial behavior from direct involvement or observation. Second, social support, which is what important others think of the individual performing the behavior, provides verbal persuasion that will encourage the entrepreneur to find starting a business either desirable or undesirable.

Both the Ajzen (1991) and Shapero (1982) models suggest that attitudes such as perceived desirability are influenced by past experiences. In addition, the influence may be greater if the past experience is with an industry related to the one the entrepreneur is considering (Brockhaus & Horwitz, 1986). Some empirical support for the influence of past experience on attitudes is found in research examining the impact of past experience on the career development of executives. For example, McCall, Lombarado, and McCauley (1988) found that many executives share attitudes based on both the breadth and quality of past experience. Smart (1989) showed a relation between life experiences and vocational choice. Krueger (1993) found limited empirical support for the role of past entrepreneurial experience in the formation of perceived desirability. Although the breadth and positiveness of past entrepreneurial experiences have been theorized as a determinant of attitudes such as perceived desirability (e.g., Martin, 1984; Moore, 1986; Krueger, 1993; Shapero, 1982; Shapero & Sokol, 1982), little empirical support is available because very few studies address the variables specifically. As a result, the current research attempts to provide support for the following theorized relations.

H2a.  The breadth of past entrepreneurial experience is positively associated with perceived desirability.

H2b.  The positiveness of past entrepreneurial experience is positively associated with perceived desirability.

Important to the formation of attitudes, such as perceived desirability of a behavior, is the perception of what others who are important to the potential entrepreneur think about him or her starting a business (Krueger et al., 1995). This concept is included in the research model as social support. Ajzen and Fishbein (1980) introduced a similar concept into their model of planned behavior as the subjective norm. They theorized that the perception of what significant others thought of an individual performing a behavior would directly influence the individual's formation of intentions. According to the theory, the more people perceive that others who are important to them think they should perform the behavior, the more they will intend to do so. Conversely, if people believe that important others think they should not perform particular behaviors, they usually will not do so (Ajzen & Fishbein, 1980).

Ajzen and Fishbein (1980) also suggested that perceptions of social support were determined not only by what significant others thought, but the willingness of the individual to comply with the wishes of the significant others. For instance, important friends may think that starting a business is not a good idea, but the individual has no motivation to comply with the wishes of the friends and starts the business anyway.

Empirical evidence for a direct influence of social support (subjective norm) on intentions has been mixed (Ajzen, 1991)(see Table 5). Recent research, however, has shown a possible indirect influence of exogenous factors such as social support on intentions through their impact on attitudes such as perceived desirability (Krueger, 1993; Scherer, Adams, Carley, & Wiebe, 1989). This new research explains why exogenous variables such as the influence of role models, have limited direct influence on entrepreneurial intentions, whereas they have significant impact on the attitudes antecedent to entrepreneurial intentions (Carsrud, Gaglio, & Olm, 1987; Krueger, 1993; Scherer et al., 1989). Based on the preceding discussion the following hypothesis is proposed.

H3. Social support is positively associated with perceived desirability.

Table 5. Summary of Research Investigating the Direct Link
Between Subjective Norm (Social Support)
and Intentions

| Study | Behaviors | Support |
|---|---|---|
| Doll & Ajzen (1990) | Playing video games | Yes |
| Watters (1989) | Participation in elections | No |
| Schifter & Ajzen (1985) | Lose weight | Yes |
| Ajzen & Madden (1986) | Attending class | No |
| Parker et al., (1990) | Commit traffic violations | Yes |
| Godin et al., (1990) | Exercising after coronary | No |
| Beale & Manstead (1991) | Limit infants' sugar intake | No |
| Krueger et al., (1995) | Entrepreneurial intentions | No |

## Propensity for Proactive Behavior and Entrepreneurial Intentions

Shapero's (1982) model suggests that it would be difficult to form intentions without a strong desire to act on them (Bagozzi & Yi, 1989). Intentions direct attention, experience, and behavior toward the accomplishment of a specific action (Bird, 1992). Therefore, the stronger a person's desire to take action, the stronger the intentions (Krueger, 1993; Shapero & Sokol, 1982). Shapero (1982) theorized that a person's propensity to act is grounded in a desire to gain control of a situation by taking action (Krueger, 1993). While new ventures are not forced into existence, they also are not the passive result of environmental conditions (Bird, 1992). New ventures are a result of planned attempts to take actions that will influence or create the environment in such a way as to allow the formation of the venture. Therefore, entrepreneurial intentions are determined by an individual's desire to take actions that will influence the environment (Crant, 1996).

The desire to take control is described by Bateman and Crant's (1993) relatively new construct of proactive behavior. They defined the "proactive personality" as a person who has a propensity for proactive behavior. Consequently, proactive behavior is a dispositional construct that identifies differences among people in the extent to which they take action to influence their environment (Bateman & Crant, 1993). It is a result of a person's need to manipulate and control the environment (Langer, 1983). The construct is rooted in the interactionist's perspective (Bandura, 1977; Schneider, 1983) that holds that behavior is both internally and externally controlled. Situations are as much a function of the individual as they are of the environment (Schneider, 1983). Bandura (1986) stated that "people create environments and set them in motion as well as rebut them" (p. 22). As a result, individuals can intentionally and directly change both their current social and nonsocial circumstances as well as the physical environment (Buss & Finn, 1987; Crant, 1996). Examples of proactive behavior are starting a new venture, solving long-range problems, and identifying a market opportunity and capitalizing on it (Bateman & Crant, 1993), all of which are important to entrepreneurship. Therefore, it is reasonable to assume that people with proactive personalities would be drawn to entrepreneurial careers (Crant, 1996).

Bateman and Crant (1993) describe the prototypic proactive personality as one who is reactively unconstrained by situational forces, and who creates environmental change. These individuals scan the environment for opportunities, show initiative, take action, and persevere until they reach closure with environmental change. They are pathfinders (Leavitt, 1988) who change the mission of their organizations and seek out and solve problems. They make it their mission to impact the world around them. On the other hand, people who are not proactive show little initiative, passively adapt to change, and even endure their circumstances. The proactive personality intuitively describes the prototypic entrepreneur.

Little research has been conducted on the proactive personality because the construct is relatively new. Bateman and Crant (1993) developed and validated a proactive personality scale. In their research, they found a proactive personality related to McCelland's need for achievement, which has been found to have a significant correlation with entrepreneurship (Brockhaus & Horwitz, 1986). In addition, Crant (1996) found a positive relationship between proactive personality and success of real estate agents (Crant, 1996). Also, Crant (1996) found a positive association between a proactive personality and the formation of entrepreneurial intentions.

In this study, it is expected that the propensity for proactive behavior, which is the tendency of a person to act in a manner consistent with a proactive personality, is positively associated with the formation of entrepreneurial intentions. As a result, the following hypothesis is proposed.

H4:   A propensity for proactive behavior is positively associated with the formation of entrepreneurial intentions.

### Entrepreneurial Self-Efficacy and Entrepreneurial Intentions

Both the "perceived behavioral control" in the Ajzen (1991) model and "perceived feasibility" in the Shapero (1982) model are constructs similar to self-efficacy (Ajzen, 1991; Krueger, 1993). Each of these variables assesses the perceived ability of the individual to successfully complete the target behavior. In fact, Krueger et al., (1995) found a positive relationship between a global measure of self-efficacy and the formation of entrepreneurial intentions.

Self-efficacy is a construct indicating that behavior, cognition, and the environment influence each other in a dynamic fashion, thus allowing individuals to form beliefs about their ability to perform specific tasks (Bandura, 1977). Unlike self-esteem, which is a judgement of self-worth, or expectancy theory's (Vroom, 1964) effort-to-performance estimate of ability to perform a narrow specific task, self-efficacy is a comprehensive summary or judgement of perceived capability of task performance (Brockner, 1988). Self-efficacy is viewed as having generative capabilities that influence a person's belief in his or capability of completing a task such as starting a firm (Bandura, 1986). Consequently, entrepreneurial self-efficacy is defined as the degree to which one believes that he or she is capable of starting a business venture.

Self-efficacy is also dynamic and changes over time as new information and experience are acquired. In addition, efficacy beliefs involve a complex and generative process, including the construction and orchestration of adaptive performance to changing circumstances (Bandura, 1988; Bandura & Wood, 1989; Gist & Mitchell, 1992). Therefore, people with the same skills may perform differently because of their efficacy beliefs. By influencing individual choices, goals, emotional reactions, effort, coping, and persistence, self-efficacy becomes a major motivational construct in determining performance (Gist & Mitchell, 1992).

Individual self-efficacy is acquired gradually through the development of complex cognitive, social, linguistic and/or physical skills through experience (Bandura, 1982). Efficacy beliefs are built and strengthened by assessing information cues. Information cues are defined as sources of experience that provide individuals with information concerning their ability to perform a specific task (Gist & Mitchell, 1992). For example, a person's perception of self-efficacy could be influenced by information gathered from his or her past experience in performing a task or by the observation of others performing the task. While cues provide important information, it is cognitive appraisal and integration of this information that ultimately determine self-efficacy (Gist, 1987). Gist and Mitchell (1992) summarize as follows: ". . . self-efficacy may be thought of as a superordinate judgement of performance capability that is induced by assimilation and integration of multiple performance determinants" (p.188).

The assimilation and integration of multiple performance determinants is accomplished by three primary assessments. First, there is an assessment of task requirements that evaluates what it takes to complete the desired behavior. Second, an assessment is made of the probability of successful performance based on the results of past experience. Finally, the individual assesses the availability of resources or the existence of possible constraints that could impact performance (Gist & Mitchell, 1992).

Previous research has shown that self-efficacy predicts motivation and task performance in a variety of work-related situations (Gist, 1987). Barling and Beattie (1983) demonstrated that self-efficacy was strongly correlated to sales performance for insurance agents. In addition, Taylor, Locke, Lee, and Gist (1984) related self-efficacy to faculty research productivity. Other areas associated with self-efficacy include coping with difficult career-related tasks (Stumpf, Brief, & Hartman, 1987), career choice (Lent, Brown, & Larkin, 1987), adaptability to new technology (Hill, Smith, & Mann, 1987) and entrepreneurial opportunity recognition (Krueger, 1989). The findings of empirical studies on self-efficacy have consistently supported its predictive ability with a variety of activities.

While self-efficacy has been shown to be a reliable predictor of behavior, the focus of this study is the self-efficacy-intentions relationship. Because of the similarity of the constructs, the relationships between Ajzen's (1991) perceived behavioral control, Shapero's (1982) perceived feasibility, and Bandura's (1982) self-efficacy with behavioral intentions all suggest support for the self-efficacy-intentions relationship. Table 6 provides examples of research that examines these relationships.

Of the three constructs, self-efficacy appears to more fully capture the complex assessments of both internal and external factors that influence behavior. It is a comprehensive summary judgement that may best describe the result of a person's mental process of determining his or her perception of successfully performing a specific task. Extending the idea further would suggest that entrepreneurial self-efficacy may be the best evaluation of the degree to which one believes that he or she is capable of starting a new business venture. Despite the empirical support and the ability of self-efficacy to capture complex assessments of both internal and external factors that influence behavior, entrepreneurial researchers have largely ignored the construct (Krueger et al., 1995). Scherer et al., (1989), however, suggest that self-efficacy is central to the formation of entrepreneurial intentions. Therefore, the study's research model includes a link between the entrepreneurial self-efficacy

## Table 6. Research in which the Self-Efficacy-Intentions Link is Examined

| Study | Intentions | Construct | Support |
|-------|-----------|-----------|---------|
| Doll & Ajzen (1990) | Play six video game | PBC | Yes |
| Watters (1989) | Participate in elections and voting choice | PBC | Yes |
| Schifter & Ajzen (1985) | Lose weight | PBC | Yes |
| Parker et al., (1990) | Commit traffic violations | PBC | Yes |
| Godin et al., (1990) | Exercise after coronary | PBC | Yes |
| Krueger (1993) | Entrepreneurial | PF | Yes |
| Krueger et al., (1995) | Entrepreneurial | PF & SE | Yes |

PBC= Perceived Behavioral Control
PF= Perceived Feasibility
SE= Self-Efficacy

construct and entrepreneurial intentions. Thus, the following hypothesis is proposed.

H5:    Entrepreneurial self-efficacy is positively associated with the formation of entrepreneurial intentions.

Entrepreneurial self-efficacy captures the interaction of environmental influences and the entrepreneur's cognitions related to his or her behavior. The interaction between the environment and the person causes the construct to be dynamic and change as new information and experience are acquired. As a result, self-efficacy judgements are formed by assessing a variety of external and internal cues (Gist & Mitchell, 1992). For example, entrepreneurial self-efficacy is formed by assessing external cues such as, resource availability and family support, and internal cues such as, perceptions of skill levels and knowledge. In addition, Weiner's (1985) research provides distinctions between the stability/instability and controllability/uncontrollability of various external and internal cues. For example, family support may be stable and controllable while resource availability may be unstable and uncontrollable.

Models of the entrepreneurial process provide numerous internal and external cues such as family support, financial support, perceptions relating to personality categories (e.g., need for achievement, risk taking propensity, locus of control), government support, and supply of venture capital (e.g., Gartner, 1985; Martin, 1984; Moore, 1986; Vesper, 1990). When the models are combined, the list of possible cues is quite extensive. The strength of self-efficacy judgements is that they allow for the assessment of the effect of the numerous internal and external cues, and associated degrees of stability and controllability on the entrepreneur's perceptions of successfully completing the formation of a business.

Bandura (1982) suggested that self-efficacy is determined by assessing information gathered from four primary sources of experience. Arranged in order from most to least influence on self-efficacy formation are enactive mastery, vicarious experience (modeling), verbal persuasion, and emotional (physiological) arousal (Bandura, 1982). Enactive mastery is the actual performance of the intended behavior. Vicarious experience is observing and modeling the performance of others. Verbal persuasion through encouraging discussion or specific performance feedback provides information useful in developing self-efficacy. Physiological arousal, which is a person's perception of his or her emotional arousal and degree of tension, provides information that is interpreted as an indication of vulnerability to poor performance (Bandura, 1982; Wood & Bandura, 1989).

The most effective way for individuals to develop strong self-efficacy judgements concerning a specific task is through repeated successful performance (enactive mastery) of the task (Bandura, 1977; Bandura, 1982; Gist & Mitchell, 1992; Wood & Bandura, 1989). Successful performance provides confirming experiences that build skills, coping abilities, and exposure needed to reinforce positive judgements of future performance (Gist, 1987). When enactive mastery is positive, it builds self-efficacy; when it is negative it lowers self-efficacy. In addition, enactive mastery developed by performing tasks that provide easy success, makes individuals more discouraged when they encounter failure. Strong self-efficacy judgements are formed when individuals overcome obstacles through effort and perseverance (Wood & Bandura, 1989). As a result, individuals who have successfully completed complex tasks associated with entrepreneurship will have stronger entrepreneurial self-efficacy judgements about future entrepreneurial ventures.

Vicarious experience, which is observational learning through modeling, is the second most effective method of formulating self-efficacy judgements (Bandura, 1977; Gist, 1987; Wood & Bandura, 1989). Individuals use the observation of role models through a social comparison process to learn ways to effectively accomplish tasks (Wood & Bandura, 1989). Individuals form judgements about their own capabilities by comparing themselves to others (Boyd & Vozikis, 1994). Through vicarious experience, individuals estimate the skills, effort, and behavior used by the role model to complete the task and then, by comparison, approximate the extent to which they have similar skills and are able to exert comparable effort to accomplish like behavior (Gist & Mitchell, 1992). Finally, the effects of vicarious experience are enhanced when the role model is perceived by the individual to have similar characteristics and capabilities (Gist, 1987).

The impact of role models on entrepreneurial activity is well established in the literature. Family and friends provide the most common role models (e.g. Brockhaus & Horwitz, 1986; Krueger et al., 1995; Shapero & Sokol, 1982). In a study conducted at Babson College, over half of the entrepreneurs produced by the school came from entrepreneurial families (Bygrave, 1997). The father appears to have the most influence on entrepreneurial activity (Litvak & Maule, 1971), especially for female entrepreneurs (Hisrich & Brush, 1984). As a result, role model research strongly suggests that role models influence the attitudes of individuals toward entrepreneurship (Krueger et al., 1995). The third source of experience that provides cues as to the strength of self-efficacy is verbal persuasion. People who receive both persuasive discussion and performance feedback use the information to form inferences about their ability to perform the task (Gist & Mitchell, 1992). Positive discussion and feedback make people more likely to exert greater effort to accomplish a task (Gist, 1987). It is important, however, to consider such factors as the credibility, expertise, trustworthiness, and the prestige of the persuading person when evaluating the information (Bandura, 1977; Gist & Mitchell, 1992). It would be reasonable, therefore, to assume that entrepreneurial activity could be influenced by positive persuasion and feedback from a person the entrepreneur respects. It should be noted, however, that this method is not as effective in forming self-efficacy judgements as either enactive mastery or vicarious experience (Gist, 1987). Finally, people often rely partly on their perceptions of physiological arousal in assessing their capabilities. They interpret their emotional state as an indication of their vulnerability to poor performance (Boyd & Vozikis, 1994). For example, anxiety concerning performing a task is often interpreted as a sign of increased likelihood of failure and will lead to lower self-efficacy judgements. (Stumpf, et al., 1987; Wood & Bandura; 1989). In addition, such factors as general physical condition, personality factors, and mood may impact self-efficacy by influencing a person's physiological arousal (Gist & Mitchell, 1992). As a result, people can increase self-efficacy by enhancing their physical and emotional condition and reducing stress levels (Gist, 1987; Wood & Bandura, 1989).

Extending this reasoning to entrepreneurial activity, entrepreneurial self-efficacy would be influenced by the emotional stress and physical demands of starting a business. The greater the level of stress, anxiety, and physical demands, the lower the judgements of entrepreneurial self-efficacy.

Gist and Mitchell (1992) propose that the informational cues gathered from the four types of experience are processed through three types of individual assessments. First, there is an assessment of task requirements, which is an evaluation of what it takes to complete the desired behavior. For example, someone wanting to develop a research proposal may consider how much statistical ability and time will be required to complete the assignment (Gist & Mitchell, 1992).

Assessment of personal and situational resources/constraints is the second type of assessment. This assessment involves a "self on setting" analysis by which the individual assesses the availability of specific resources and the existence of constraints that could impact performance (Gist & Mitchell, 1992). For example, consider again the example of the research proposal. The individual decides that a high level of statistical ability is required to complete the research project. In addition, the time required is considerable. This assessment would involve a judgement of the individual's statistical ability in relation to what is required and the amount of available time he or she has to spend on the project in comparison to what is required. If the individual decides that he or she has sufficient statistical ability and sufficient time, then self-efficacy concerning the project will be high.

Attributional analysis of experience is the third type of assessment. Individuals form judgements or attributions about why a particular past performance level occurred and then attribute the potential for success to the present task (Gist & Mitchell, 1992). Following the previous example, a successful research proposal completed in the past is attributed to the individual's statistical skill and hard work. This strengthens the self-efficacy judgements of successfully completing the new project. For novel projects, however, where the individual has little or no direct experience, this assessment may be of less importance than the other two assessments (Gist & Mitchell, 1992). For many people, starting an entrepreneurial venture may be a situation where they have little or no past experience.

Gist and Mitchell (1992) proposed that these three assessments are relatively independent. Progression through them, however, may occur in an iterative manner. The relative importance placed on each assessment may be related to past experience or to the specific nature of the task. For novel task situations, self-efficacy is formed primarily through assessment of task requirements and personal and situational resources and constraints (Gist & Mitchell, 1992). Because starting an entrepreneurial venture is a novel task for many, there will be a greater reliance on the assessment of the task requirements for starting a business coupled with an assessment of personal and situational resources and constraints related to starting a venture.

Based on the previous research, the research model suggests that entrepreneurial self-efficacy is formed by three primary determinants (Figure 3). First, entrepreneurial self-efficacy is formed by the extent (breadth) and, second, by the positiveness of a person's past entrepreneurial experience. The third determinant is a self-efficacy assessment that is the result of the iterative process of assessing task requirements for starting a venture coupled with the person's assessment of available resources/constraints and his or her ability to successfully complete the start-up tasks.

The breadth of past entrepreneurial experience is determined by the amount of exposure to past enactive mastery, vicarious experience, verbal persuasion, and physiological arousal. In addition, the impact of past experience may be more pronounced if the experience is in an industry similar to the one the entrepreneur is considering (Brockhaus & Horwitz, 1986). The most likely exposure will come from one's family business, a business started by another relative or friend, working in someone's business or starting one's own business (Krueger, 1993). While some individuals will have enactive mastery experience from starting a business or working in one, many will rely more heavily on vicarious experience, verbal persuasion, and physiological arousal derived from a family business or one started by a friend or relative. The information is provided primarily by observing and listening to role models (e.g., family and friends) in each of these situations (e.g., Brockhaus & Horwitz, 1996; Bygrave, 1997; Krueger, 1993; Shapero & Sokol, 1982). These experiences will influence the development of entrepreneurial self-efficacy. Therefore, the following hypothesis is suggested.

H6a:   The breadth of past entrepreneurial experience is positively associated with entrepreneurial self-efficacy.

Not only will the quantity (breadth) of past experience influence entrepreneurial self-efficacy, but so will the quality (i.e., positive or negative) (Krueger, 1993). The most effective way for individuals to develop strong self-efficacy judgements is through repeated successful performance of the task or through positive reinforcement from vicarious experience, verbal persuasion, and physiological arousal (Bandura, 1977; Bandura, 1982; Gist & Mitchell, 1992; Bandura & Wood, 1989). Positive exposure provides confirming experiences that build skills, coping abilities, and reinforces judgements of future performance (Gist, 1987). Therefore, positive past entrepreneurial experience will strengthen entrepreneurial self-efficacy. As a result, the following hypothesis is suggested.

H6b:   The positiveness of past entrepreneurial experience is positively associated with entrepreneurial self-efficacy.

During the self-efficacy assessment, the potential entrepreneur will first determine what tasks are involved and the degree of importance of each task for successfully starting a new venture. Second, the entrepreneur will assess his or her ability to complete the task along with the availability of any resources necessary for successful entrepreneurial behavior (Gist & Mitchell, 1992). If the potential entrepreneur feels that he or she has the ability and resources necessary to successfully start a new venture, entrepreneurial self-efficacy will be enhanced. The opposite will be true for individuals who perceive a lack of resources and ability to complete the necessary tasks. Therefore, the following hypothesis is proposed.

H7.  Self-efficacy assessment is positively associated with entrepreneurial self-efficacy.

## The Moderating Effect of a Trigger Event

Individuals are held on a given life path by the inertia of their daily lives (Shapero & Sokol, 1982). People tend to build stable life structures that they are reluctant to change (Levinson, 1978). The reluctance to change stems from motivational barriers such as the pain of loss, uncertainty, fear of failure (Levinson, 1978), and feelings of obligation to maintain the current situation (e.g., Levinson, 1978; Tushman & Romanelli, 1985). The decision to break the inertia can come gradually from an accumulation of factors (e.g., general job dissatisfaction) or abruptly as the result of a "trigger event" (e.g., marriage, loss of a job, missed promotion).

One area of life in which the trigger event is often present is an individual's decision to change careers (Osipow & Fitzgerald, 1996). Research by Baucus and Human (1994) found that the decision to make entrepreneurship a career choice is not only the result of a gradual change process, but is many times the result of a displacing trigger event. Therefore, the decision to become an entrepreneur could involve incremental cumulative change, or be triggered by an abrupt shift between periods of inertia and periods of dynamic change in a person's life (Dyer, 1992; Gersick, 1991; Quinn, 1980; Van de Ven, 1992). As a result, the idea of a trigger event has found its way into the entrepreneurial process models developed by several researchers (e.g., Bygrave, 1997; Martin, 1984; Shapero, 1975; Shapero & Sokol, 1982). While the concept of a trigger event is found in many of the conceptual models of entrepreneurship, there is very little empirical evidence to support the idea. Table 7 provides examples of research concerning the impact of trigger events.

The trigger event could result from negative changes (e.g., job loss) or positive changes (e.g., marriage). Research has shown that

*The Formation of Entrepreneurial Intentions*

**Table 7. Research that Supports the Concept of a Trigger Event in the Entrepreneurial Decision**

| Study | Empirical | Conceptual |
|---|---|---|
| Baucus & Human (1994) | X | |
| Boswell (1972) | X | |
| Bygrave (1997) | | X |
| Carroll (1965) | X | |
| Dyer (1992) | | X |
| Martin (1984) | | X |
| Moore (1986) | | X |
| Shapero (1975) | X | |
| Shapero & Sokol (1982) | | X |

negative events have more impact on the entrepreneurial decision than positive events (Shapero & Sokol, 1982). For example, Shapero (1975) reported that in a study of 109 entrepreneurs, 65% reported the sole or primary displacement that caused them to start a business was negative while 28% reported a positive displacement. Only five percent of the entrepreneurs indicated that they slowly realized they wanted to start a new firm. A variety of similar studies confirm the influence of negative triggers (e.g., Boswell, 1972; Baucus & Human, 1994; Carroll).

Negative displacements that trigger entrepreneurial activity can result from the extremes of war and political upheaval to a more subtle sense of general job dissatisfaction (Shapero, 1975). Interestingly, research on political refugees indicates that refugees tend to start a large number of businesses in their new home country (Bonifay, Eon, Labre, & Meler, 1974). For the average individual, however, displacements are far less dramatic. Job-related displacements are by far the most common (Shapero & Sokol, 1982). Loss of job, a missed promotion, a sense of boredom, company reorganization, a perception of lost career opportunity, and transfers are all examples of job-related triggers. All of these have the potential to prompt entrepreneurial behaviors.

Some negative displacements are not job-related and often are internally generated such as a "traumatic birthday" or reaching a certain stage of life development (Levinson, 1978). Others are a result of changing patterns in one's life. Divorce, death of a spouse, or just being in a state of flux, such as after graduation from school or discharge from the military, are examples of negative displacements. These dislocations tend to disturb the stable life structures and cause individuals to enter transitional periods (Levinson, 1978). From a career perspective, these transition periods may lead to a choice of an entrepreneurial venture (Shapero & Sokol, 1982).

Displacements also may be positive. Events such as marriage, birth of a child, offer of financial support, and encouragement from a trusted mentor or role model may serve as triggers to pull a person away from life's stable structures (Shapero, 1975).

One of the more powerful of the positive pulls is the encouragement of a mentor. Shapero (1975) reported that in a number of interviews with entrepreneurs, the encouragement of a mentor greatly influenced their decision to start a business. In addition, Levinson (1978) suggested that in times of transition, people tend to form special relationships with outsiders from whom they gain encouragement and learn new ways to live. The cognitive confusion and emotional distress created by major transition makes people particularly receptive to the outside influence of a mentor. The benefits provided by the outside mentor may include new cognitive perspectives, fresh awareness about the environment, and an energizing reassurance (Gersick, 1991)

The decision to change a deep-rooted life pattern and possibly start a business could result from the extra push of a trigger event or develop slowly over a period of time. Gersick (1991), however, also proposed that the trigger event itself may not be enough to cause change. Instead, the timing of the event determines the perceived significance and its potential to influence change (Gersick, 1991). Therefore, a trigger event combined with an individual's perception that there are deficiencies in his or her life and that there are corrective alternatives, could cause an individual to change. Extending this reasoning to the research model implies that a trigger event combined with high perceptions of desirability, entrepreneurial self-efficacy, and propensity for proactive behavior could enhance the formation of entrepreneurial intentions. Conversely, it is possible to develop entrepreneurial intentions slowly over time without a trigger event. Therefore, the following hypothesis is proposed.

H8:   The existence of a trigger event will moderate the relation-
      ships between perceived desirability, entrepreneurial self-
      efficacy, and propensity for proactive behavior and entrepre-
      neurial intentions. That is, the presence of a trigger event
      will strengthen the relationships between perceived desir-
      ability, propensity for proactive behavior, and entrepreneurial
      self-efficacy, and entrepreneurial intentions.

## CHAPTER SUMMARY

The first part of this chapter provided a review of the literature
that investigates the ability of intentions to predict behavior. The
research indicates that if certain assumptions and conditions are met
(i.e., behavior is under volitional control, a perception that the
chances of success are good, a correspondence exists between
measures of intentions and behavior, and measures remain stable
during the time between when intentions and behavior are measured), intentions are one of the best predictors of behavior. This was
followed by a discussion of the application of the four assumptions
to the entrepreneurial intentions-behavior relationship.

The next section examined the literature that describes the
nature of intentions. The findings indicate that intentions are able
to capture the link between the individual and his or her actions.
Next, research was presented that successfully used intentions-
based models as the primary theoretical framework to guide the
studies.

The subsequent section introduced Ajzen's (1991) theory of
planned behavior as a widely used intentions-based model.
Research was presented that confirmed the influence of a person's
attitude toward a behavior and perceived behavioral control on the
formation of intentions. In addition, research confirmed predictive
ability of the intentions-behavior relationship.

The next section discussed Shapero's (1982) intentions-based
model of the entrepreneurial event. Strong empirical support was
presented for the influence of perceived desirability, perceived feasibility, and a propensity to take action on the formation of entrepreneurial intentions. Results of research that simultaneously
tested the Ajzen (1991) and Shapero (1982) models were then presented. Overall, the Shapero (1982) model was shown to be the
more robust for predicting entrepreneurial intentions.

The final major section introduces the research model used in the study. The model indicates that perceived desirability, propensity for proactive behavior, and entrepreneurial self-efficacy are directly related to the formation of entrepreneurial intentions. The relationships, however, are moderated by the existence of some trigger event. The research that was presented indicates that the trigger is most often a negative rather than a positive event in a person's life. The model also indicates that perceived desirability is influenced by social support and the breadth and positiveness of past entrepreneurial experience. Finally, the model suggests that entrepreneurial self-efficacy is influenced by a self-efficacy assessment and the breadth and positiveness of past entrepreneurial experience. The concluding sections of the chapter described the theoretical support and eight proposed hypotheses for the relationships suggested in the model.

## CHAPTER III

# Method

This chapter presents the research procedure and methodology for the current study. A discussion of the sample is presented, followed by a description of the study's data collection method. Finally, a discussion of the variables and the specific instruments used to measure these variables including the results of a pilot study used to assess their initial reliability was presented.

## SAMPLE

Gartner (1989) stated that a persistent weakness of research into the determinants of entrepreneurial intentions is the inability to select a sample that includes individuals serious about entrepreneurship, who are in the process of making the decision to become involved in creating a new business. Most studies include samples of individuals who have already started a business or graduating college seniors who may or may not be serious about entrepreneurship. To address this weakness, the sample for this study consisted of 125 students at a small Texas junior college of which 56 were in the process of making a decision about becoming a real estate agent and 69 were interested in career development but not necessarily real estate. The 56 students interested in real estate were enrolled in any of the following three real estate courses required for licensing as a real estate agent: real estate principles, real estate contracts, or the law of agency. Sixty-nine of the respondents were drawn from courses designed to enhance career development, but not directed at entrepreneurship (i.e., organization behavior, human resource management). All of the students were enrolled in courses that were conducted either at night or on the weekend. The night and weekend formats tend to attract older and more experienced people who are serious about developing their career. Day classes were not part of the sample because they tend to attract students who are enrolled in the classes only to meet degree requirements and are not enrolled to satisfy requirements for a real estate license or develop their current career.

Overall, this provided a sample with 56 students in the process of making the decision to engage in the entrepreneurial activity of becoming a real estate agent and 69 engaged in career development, but not necessarily real estate. The inclusion of both types of subjects was done to ensure variance in the measures related to the formation of entrepreneurial intentions.

Prior research has indicated that personal characteristics, such as education level, age, gender, and the quantity of past work experience, could influence entrepreneurial behavior (Brockhaus & Horwitz, 1986). Consequently, it is desirable that the real estate and non-real estate subjects be as similar in these characteristics as possible. The night and weekend course formats tend to attract individuals who are similar in the critical demographic factors. The pilot study conducted prior to the research confirmed this assumption by finding that the real estate and non-real estate subjects were similar in age, years of work experience, level of education, and gender.

Results from the current study, however, indicated that the two types of respondents were dissimilar according to age and level of education. The real estate portion of the sample was older and had a greater proportion with college degrees (see Table 8). As a result, age and level of education were included in the analysis of the data to control for any effects they may have.

Texas law requires that a person must be associated with a licensed broker in order to be a real estate agent. The relationship created between the broker and the sales agent usually takes the form of independent contractor. Nance (1996) states that independent contractor status allows the broker to guide the activities of the sales agent, but not tell the agent when or how to do the job. Essentially, the agent is an independent business person who is responsible for paying his or her own income and self employment tax and, in addition, assumes the business risk of making a profit or not. The Internal Revenue Service (IRS) requires independent contractors to

**Table 8. Comparison of Real Estate vs. Non-Real Estate Respondents**

| Characteristic | Real Estate | Non-Real Estate | Test Statistic |
|---|---|---|---|
| Average Age (years) | 39.2 | 33.9 | $t = 2.74$** |
| Level of Education (Number in each level) | | | |
|   High School | 9 | 3 | |
|   Some College | 24 | 46 | |
|   College Degree | 23 | 20 | $\chi^2 = 13.36$* |
| Gender (Number) | | | |
|   Male | 24 | 21 | |
|   Female | 32 | 48 | $\chi^2 = 1.87$ |
| Average Years of Work Experience | 16.6 | 13.7 | $t = 1.5$ |

n = 125
* $p < .05$
** $p < .01$

report income/losses and expenses in the same manner as any independent business owner. Overall, the IRS treats independent contractors like independent business owners. Therefore, real estate sales agents satisfy the study's definition of entrepreneurship: starting an independent profit-making business venture (Bird, 1989). Consequently, individuals preparing to become real estate agents are in the process of making an entrepreneurial decision.

## PROCEDURE

The instructor for each of the classes used in the study was contacted and permission gained for the researcher to collect the data in person. Consequently, the data were collected by the researcher during scheduled class meetings by having the students respond to a packet containing demographic questions and a questionnaire to assess the independent and dependent variables in the study. Because some students were enrolled in more than one class, they were instructed that if they had already completed the questionnaire they should not do so again. Also, any student who was already licensed as a real estate agent was asked not to participate. Next, the researcher explained the consent statement required for the use of human subjects as a condition for approval of the research study by the University of North Texas , covered the beginning instructions, asked for volunteers to provide addresses and telephone numbers for a post hoc follow up, and then asked the students to provide the information requested. In addition, students were reminded that all information given was to be held in confidence. Each questionnaire was checked to ensure all information had been given. Once the information had been gathered, subjects were provided a debriefing statement, and any questions they had were answered.

## MEASURES

### Entrepreneurial Intentions

Entrepreneurial intentions were measured with a single-item question asking respondents to choose a probability, from 0% to 100%, that they would take the Texas real estate license exam in the near future (Section 4, Appendix). The scale was developed using a format suggested by Ajzen and Fishbein (1980). The higher the probability indicated, the stronger the intentions to become a real estate agent.

Taking the Texas Real Estate License Exam was selected as the target behavior of intentions because of the uniqueness of Texas law. Texas law requires that an individual desiring to become a real estate agent must take and pass the state license exam. To be eligible to take the exam, an individual must establish a relationship with a sponsoring licensed real estate broker. In fact, the sponsoring broker must request permission from the state for the potential agent to take the exam. In other words, an agent cannot take the license exam and then decide to start a real estate business. The decision must be made before the exam is taken. Therefore, taking the license exam is a critical point in becoming an agent, and is an indication of the individual's commitment to the physical creation of his or her business. This is consistent with Behave's (1994) suggestion that "starting" a business is best indicated by a behavior that shows commitment to physical creation.

## Perceived Desirability

Perceived desirability for starting a business was defined for the current study ". . . as the degree to which one finds the prospect of starting a business to be attractive; in essence, it reflects one's affect toward entrepreneurship" (Krueger, 1993, p. 8). Three questions developed by Shapero (1982) and two additional questions developed for the purpose of this study were used to assess perceived desirability. Responses were gathered on a 7-point Likert scale ranging from 1 = a negative perception to 7 = a positive perception (Section 2, Appendix). Total scale scores were obtained by summing the five questions.

Krueger (1993) reported a Cronbach's alpha of .77 for the three-item scale developed by Shapero (1982) (items 1,2, and 3) and in a similar study, Krueger et al., (1995) reported a Cronbach's alpha of .69 for the same scale. A pilot study conducted prior to the research produced an alpha of .68 for Shapero's three items. As a result, two additional questions were developed and added to the current study (items 4 and 5) to improve the overall reliability of the measure. The current study produced Cronbach's alpha of .85 for the five-item scale.

## Propensity for Proactive Behavior

For this study, propensity for proactive behavior was defined as the tendency of individuals to act in a way consistent with a proactive personality. The proactive personality is someone who identifies opportunities and acts on them; the person shows initiative, takes action, and perseveres until it changes the environment (Crant, 1996).

The construct was measured by a 17-item proactive personality scale developed and validated by Bateman and Crant (1993) (Section 1, Appendix). Responses were obtained on a 7-point Likert scale ranging from 1 = strongly disagree to 7 = strongly agree. The total score was determined by summing responses to the individual items. The higher the sum, the greater the propensity for proactive behavior.

In Bateman and Crant's (1993) validation study, they found high internal reliability (coefficient alpha ranging from .87 to .89) and reasonable test-retest reliabilities of .72 for the measure. In addition, the proactive personality scale showed significant criterion validities. In a pilot study, the scale had an alpha of .91. Data from the current study produced an alpha of .89 which is consistent with the range of alpha found by Bateman and Crant (1993).

## Entrepreneurial Self-efficacy

For the current study, entrepreneurial self-efficacy was defined as the degree to which one believes that he or she is capable of successfully starting a new venture. Successfully starting a real estate business involves being able to sell real estate. Respondents were asked to evaluate their capability for selling varying amounts of real estate. For example, they were asked to evaluate their chances of selling real estate at levels ranging from $500,000 to $10,0000,000. The individual levels correspond to the various levels of sales recognized for special awards by the local board of Realtors (Section 8, Appendix). This approach to assessing self-efficacy is consistent with earlier research (e.g., Bandura, 1986; Gist & Mitchell, 1992; Locke, Frederick, Lee, & Bobko, 1984).

The scale is designed to measure both the magnitude and strength of entrepreneurial self-efficacy as suggested by Gist and Mitchell (1992). Magnitude is measured by dichotomous (yes or no) responses to questions assessing the respondent's capability for selling real estate at various levels. Traditionally, the magnitude score is the number of "yes" responses (Bandura, 1986). Respondents are then asked to rate from 0% to 100% their confidence that their "yes" or "no" responses are accurate. The total strength of entrepreneurial self-efficacy is the sum of the confidence responses for all "yes" responses (Locke, Frederick, Lee, & Bobko, 1984).

Lee and Bobko (1994) conducted a study that compared five measures of self-efficacy, and found that a composite measure of magnitude and strength provided the best results. Therefore, for this study, a composite score was used. This score was the sum of the confidence responses on the levels that received a "yes" answer. The higher the composite score, the greater the entrepreneurial self-efficacy.

The scale was included in the pilot study conducted prior to the research. The construction of the scale does not allow for the determination of coefficient alpha. Respondents in the pilot study, however, did not report any confusion or other problems with the scale.

## Trigger Event

Shapero (1975) suggested that entrepreneurial activity is often triggered by an event that disrupts or displaces human inertia. This event can either be positive (e.g., marriage) or negative (e.g., job loss). For this study, trigger event was defined as an event (either positive or negative) that disrupts or displaces the inertia of human behavior.

The four most common sources of trigger events are changes in life situations (e.g., marriage, divorce, graduation), changes in work situations (e.g., promotion, loss of job, missed raise), changes in career prospects (e.g., better opportunity, less opportunity, desire for change), and the pull of a mentor (Levinson, 1978; Shapero, 1975; Shapero & Sokol, 1982). Trigger event was measured by four dichotomous (yes or no) questions asking about changes in life situations, work situations, career prospects, and pull of a mentor (Section 7, Appendix). For each question with a "yes" response, the respondent was asked, "If yes, how much have these changes influenced your life?" Responses were obtained on a four-point scale ranging from 1 = not at all to 4 = strongly. The total score was the sum of the degree of influence for all questions answered "yes." The greater the total for the degree of influence, the more likely a trigger event could have an impact.

The scale used was developed specifically for the current study. In the pilot study, respondents were asked only the four dichotomous (yes/no) questions. As a result of the pilot, it was decided to add the degree of influence to each question to provide greater variance in the responses. Because subjects indicated a degree of influence for the "yes" responses only, reliability calculations could not be completed.

## Self-efficacy Assessment

Gist and Mitchell (1992) suggest that self-efficacy judgements are partially determined by an assessment of task requirements coupled with an assessment of the availability of resources/constraints and individual skills necessary to successfully complete the task. For the current study, self-efficacy assessment was defined as an individual's assessment of what it takes to start a business coupled with perceived availability of resources/constraints and skills necessary to successfully complete the task.

To develop a measure, two top producing real estate sales agents were each asked to make a list of the skills, abilities, and resources that he or she felt were necessary for success in real estate. Then, the agents were asked to examine each other's list and agree on a final set of necessary skills, abilities, and resources. They agreed on 15 items that were used as the basis for the measure of self-efficacy assessment (Section 5, Appendix). For each of the 15 items, subjects responded to a pair of questions. In the first question of each pair, respondents were asked to rate on a 7-point Likert scale the importance of the specific skill or resource identified in the base item for success as a real estate agent. The scale ranged from 1 = not important to 7 = very important. In the second question, respondents were asked if they had sufficient ability to perform the skill or sufficient quantity of the resource identified in the base item. Responses were obtained on a 7-point Likert scale ranging from 1 = very little (or not enough) to 7 = more than enough. The score on the first and second question of each pair were multiplied together. The total self-efficacy assessment score was the sum of the products of the 15 pairs of questions. The higher the total score, the greater the perception that the individual has of what it takes to successfully become a real estate agent.

The scale was developed specifically for the current study and was based on two assessments suggested by Gist and Mitchell (1992). Gist and Mitchell (1992) suggested that self-efficacy was determined by assessing what it takes (i.e., skills, abilities, resources) to do a specific task along with an assessment of whether a person has the required skills, abilities, and resources necessary to do what it takes. The 15 pairs of questions were developed to capture these two assessments.

The scale was used in the pilot study and produced a reliability coefficient alpha of .94. Data from the current study produced a reliability coefficient alpha of .93.

## Breadth and Positiveness of Past Entrepreneurial Experience

The breadth and positiveness of past entrepreneurial experience was defined for the study as the extent to which a person has been exposed to entrepreneurship (real estate) in the past and whether the past experiences are perceived as positive or negative. The variables was measured on scales developed by Krueger (1993). These scales were modified to be real estate specific (Section 3, Appendix). Breadth of past experience was measured by asking subjects whether they had been exposed to each of four types of entrepreneurial experience (Krueger, 1993). Breadth of experience is the sum of the four "yes"-"no" questions (coded 1 for yes, 0 for no).

Positiveness of past entrepreneurial experience was measured by asking subjects, after each of the four breadth questions that were answered "yes," to rate the experience as positive or negative. Positive responses were coded 1 and negative responses were coded 0. Positiveness of experience is the sum of each of these items (Krueger, 1993). Because respondents were asked to rate positiveness of past experience as either positive or negative only for those situations for which they had experience, the calculation for internal reliability was not meaningful.

## Social Support

Ajzen and Fishbein (1980) suggest that social support is a perception of what important people (e.g., family, friends) in the life of a potential entrepreneur think about him or her starting a business coupled with the entrepreneur's desire to comply with the wishes of the important others. Consequently, social support was defined as an individual's perception of what important others think of an individual starting a business venture and the motivation of the individual to comply with the wishes of the important others.

Social support was measured on a scale format suggested by Ajzen (1991) and Ajzen and Fishbein, (1980)(Section 6, Appendix). First, individuals were asked to rate, on a 7-point Likert scale, what their family or friends would think if they started a real estate business. The scale responses ranged from 1 = I should (coded +3) to 7 = I should not (coded –3). Second, each question was followed by a query asking the respondent to express his or her motivation to comply with the wishes of family and friends on a 4-point scale (1 = not at all motivated, 4 = strongly motivated). The total score is the sum of each of the item products of the important others scale and the corresponding motivation to comply scale [i.e., (question 1a × question 1b) + (question 2a × question 2b); see Section 6, Appendix].

The scale was used in the pilot study and resulted in an internal reliability coefficient alpha of .76. The reliability coefficient alpha for the current study was .81.

## CHAPTER SUMMARY

This chapter presented a description of the study's sample consisting of 56 respondents from real estate classes required for licensing and 69 from other career development classes. This was followed by a discussion of the procedure. The next section described each of the measures including scoring techniques and the results of the pilot conducted to obtain support for use of measures developed or altered for this research. Coefficient alphas were presented where applicable.

## CHAPTER IV

# Results

This chapter contains the results of the data analyses used to test the hypothesized relationships in this study. A correlation matrix of the primary variables included in the research model is provided first, with the mean, standard deviation and reliability coefficients for each variable also included. The following sections describe the hierarchical regression procedure used to test each hypothesis and the results of each test.

## CORRELATIONS

Table 9 contains descriptive statistics and correlations among all measured variables in the study. Reliabilities are presented on the diagonal. These data were collected from all 125 respondents in the sample.

## HYPOTHESES

Hierarchical regression was the primary method of analysis used to test the hypotheses in the study. Cohen and Cohen (1983) suggest this method is most important when independent variables possess a theoretically-based casual priority.

The hierarchical regression procedure was used to test three separate paths in the research model. The first path (shaded area Figure 4) included the relationship between social support, breadth and positiveness of past entrepreneurial experience, perceived desirability, and entrepreneurial intentions including the moderating

**Table 9. Descriptive Statistics and Correlation Matrix Among Variables in Research Model**

| | Mean | s.d. | 1 | 2 | 3 | 4 | 5 | 6 | 7 | 8 | 9 | 10 |
|---|---|---|---|---|---|---|---|---|---|---|---|---|
| 1. Age | 36.37 | 11.07 | | | | | | | | | | |
| 2. [1]BPEE | 3.61 | 1.90 | .24** | | | | | | | | | |
| 3. [2]ED | 3.53 | 1.06 | .31** | .20 | | | | | | | | |
| 4. [3]EI | 47.83 | 44.42 | .14 | .39** | .11 | | | | | | | |
| 5. [4]PD | 23.94 | 7.82 | .02 | .22* | -.08 | .59** | (.85) | | | | | |
| 6. [5]PPB | 90.86 | 12.75 | .09 | .25** | .08 | .26** | .33** | (.89) | | | | |
| 7. [6]PPEE | 3.87 | 2.86 | .08 | .71** | .10 | .33** | .30** | .29** | | | | |
| 8. [7]ESE | 164.55 | 172.78 | .13 | .22** | .10 | .40** | .42** | .37** | .24** | | | |
| 9. [8]SEA | 459.02 | 144.51 | .22* | .32** | .12 | .61** | .67** | .44** | .42** | .48** | (.87) | |
| 10. [9]SS | 1.90 | 7.48 | .12 | .16 | -.10 | .39** | .34** | .23** | .21* | .23** | .42** | (.81) |
| 11. [10]TE | 7.44 | 4.02 | .03 | .26** | -.03 | .36** | .22** | .27** | .22* | .21* | .33** | .17 |

n = 125

* $p < .05$

** $p < .01$

( ) Cronbach's alpha coefficients

[1]BPEE - Breadth of Past Entrepreneurial Experience

[2]Ed - Education

[3]EI - Entrepreneurial Intentions

[4]PD - Perceived Desirability

[5]PPB - Propensity for Proactive Behavior

[6]PPEE - Positiveness of Past Entrepreneurial Experience

[7]ESE - Entrepreneurial Self-Efficacy

[8]SEA - Self-Efficacy Assessment

[9]SS - Social Support

[10]TE - Trigger Event

## Figure 4. Path I Analysis

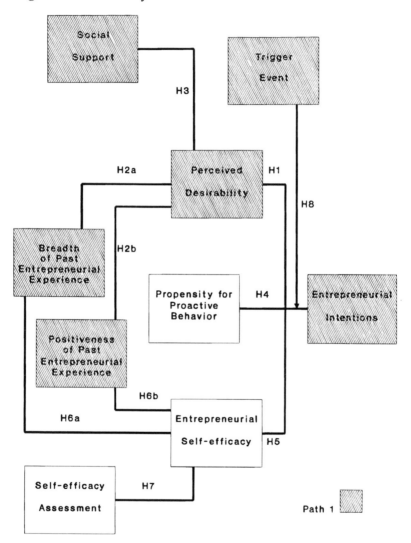

impact of a trigger event (hypotheses 1, 2a, 2b, 3, and part of 8). The second path (shaded area Figure 5) included the relationship between propensity for proactive behavior and entrepreneurial intentions (hypothesis H4), along with the moderating effect of a trigger event (part of hypothesis H8). The third path (shaded area Figure 6) included the relationship between breadth and positiveness of past entrepreneurial experience, self-efficacy assessment, entrepreneurial self-efficacy, and entrepreneurial intentions, including the moderating effect of a trigger event (hypotheses 5, 6a, 6b, 7, and part of 8). In each path, age and level of education were included as the first step in the procedure to control for any effects they may have had on the proposed relationships.

Path I was tested using a two-phase hierarchical regression procedure. Phase 1 was done in two steps (Table 10). In step 1, age and level of education were the independent variables and perceived desirability was the dependent variable. This approach was taken to control for any effect they may have had on the relationships. For step 2, social support, breadth of past entrepreneurial experience, and positiveness of past entrepreneurial experience were added to the regression equation as independent variables and perceived desirability was entered as the dependent variable. The significance of the $F$ test statistic and the change in $R^2$ were tested to assess the contribution of adding the variables (Phedhazur & Schmelkin, 1991). All variables in this step were entered at once because there is no theoretical support for entering the variables in any specific order. The sign and significance of each Beta (standardized regression coefficient) in the regression equation were used to test the hypotheses. A positive sign and a significant Beta would provide support for the hypotheses (H3, H2a, H2b).

A potential threat to the analysis in phase 1 was presence of multicollinearity among the independent variables. Highly correlated independent variables could cause the sign and significance of the individual Betas to be uninterpretable (Neter, Wasserman, & Kunter, 1990). Some of the correlations presented in Table 9 were significant, thus, causing concern for the negative effects of multicollinearity on the results.

To assess the impact of multicollinearity on the phase 1 results, the variance inflation factor (VIF) technique of testing for the influence of multicollinearity was used. A VIF greater than 10 indicates

# Figure 5. Path II Analysis

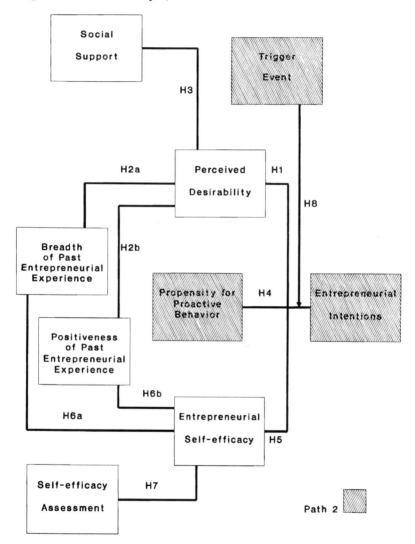

**Figure 6. Path III Analysis**

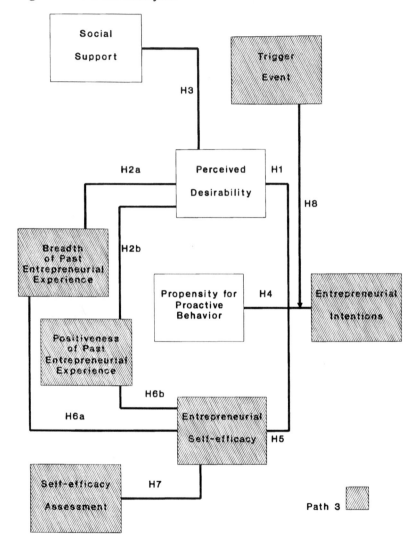

**Table 10. Outline of Path I Analysis**

| Regression | Dependent Variable | Independent Variables Entered |
|---|---|---|
| Phase 1 | | |
|   Step 1 | Perceived Desirability | Age, Education |
|   Step 2 | Perceived Desirability | SS[1], BPEE[2], PPEE[3] |
| Phase 2 | | |
|   Step 1 | Entrepreneurial Intentions | Age, Education |
|   Step 2 | Entrepreneurial Intentions | SS[1], BPEE[2], PPEE[3] |
|   Step 3 | Entrepreneurial Intentions | PD[4] |
|   Step 4 | Entrepreneurial Intentions | TE[5] |
|   Step 5 | Entrepreneurial Intentions | (TExPD)[6] |

[1] SS - Social Support
[2] BPEE - Breadth of Past Entrepreneurial Experience
[3] PPEE - Positiveness of Past Entrepreneurial Experience
[4] PD - Perceived Desirability
[5] TE - Trigger Event
[6] (TExPD) - Interaction of Trigger Event and Perceived Desirability

the presence of a multicollinearity problem (Mendenhall & Sincich, 1989). No VIFs greater than 10 were found.

In phase 2 of the Path I analysis, the variables of interest were entered into a series of regression equations in a five step process (Table 10). The change in $R^2$ was tested for significance to assess the contribution of adding the variables (Pedhazur & Schmelkin, 1991). In each step of the process, entrepreneurial intentions was the dependent variable. Age and level of education were the independent variables in step 1 and were used as control variables. The hierarchical regression procedure continued with the addition of breadth of past entrepreneurial, the positiveness of past entrepreneurial experience, and social support (step 2), perceived desirability (step 3), trigger event (step 4), and the interaction of trigger event and perceived desirability (step 5). A significant change in $R^2$ for step 3 provides support for the association between perceived desirability and entrepreneurial intentions (H1). A significant change in $R^2$ as the interaction term was entered (step 5), provides support for the moderating effect of a trigger event on the relationship between perceived desirability and entrepreneurial intentions (part of H8).

Path II was tested using a single-phase, four step, procedure to test the association between propensity for proactive behavior and entrepreneurial intentions (H4) and the moderating effect of a trigger event on the relationship between entrepreneurial intentions and propensity for proactive behavior (part of H8) (Table 11). In all steps, entrepreneurial intentions was the dependent variable. In step 1, age and level of education were entered as control variables. Next, propensity for proactive behavior was entered (step 2), followed by trigger event (step 3). The procedure ended with the addition of the interaction between trigger event and propensity for

**Table 11. Outline of Path II Analysis**

| Regression | Dependent Variable | Independent Variables Entered |
|---|---|---|
| Phase 1 | | |
| Step 1 | Entrepreneurial Intentions | Age, Education |
| Step 2 | Entrepreneurial Intentions | PPB[1] |
| Step 3 | Entrepreneurial Intentions | TE[2] |
| Step 4 | Entrepreneurial Intentions | (TExPPB)[3] |

[1] PPB - Propensity for Proactive Behavior
[2] TE - Trigger Event
[3] (TExPPB) - Interaction of Trigger Event and Propensity for Proactive Behavior

proactive behavior (step 5). A significant change in $R^2$ in step 2 provides support for H4 and a significant increase in $R^2$, as the interaction was entered (step 5), indicates support for part of H8.

Finally, Path III was tested using a two-phase hierarchical regression procedure similar to the one used to test Path I (Table 12). Phase 1 of Path III was done in two steps. In step 1, age and education were entered as the independent variables and entrepreneurial self-efficacy was the independent variable. As was the case in phase 1 of Path I, this was done to control for any effect they may

## Table 12. Outline of Path III Analysis

| Regression | Dependent Variable | Independent Variables Entered |
|---|---|---|
| Phase 1 | | |
| Step 1 | Entrepreneurial Self-efficacy | Age, Education |
| Step 2 | Entrepreneurial Self-efficacy | SEA[1], BPEE[2], PPEE[3] |
| Phase 2 | | |
| Step 1 | Entrepreneurial Intentions | Age, Education |
| Step 2 | Entrepreneurial Intentions | SEA[1], BPEE[2], PPEE[3] |
| Step 3 | Entrepreneurial Intentions | ESE[4] |
| Step 4 | Entrepreneurial Intentions | TE[5] |
| Step 5 | Entrepreneurial Intentions | (TExESE)[6] |

[1] SEA - Self-efficacy Assessment
[2] BPEE - Breadth of Past Entrepreneurial Experience
[3] PPEE - Positiveness of Past Entrepreneurial Experience
[4] ESE - Entrepreneurial Self-efficacy
[5] TE - Trigger Event
[6] (TExPD) - Interaction of Trigger Event and Entrepreneurial Self-efficacy

have had on the relationships. For step 2, breadth of past entrepreneurial experience, positiveness of past entrepreneurial experience, and self-efficacy assessment were entered as independent variables and entrepreneurial self-efficacy was entered as the dependent variable. The significance of the $F$ test statistic and the change in $R^2$ were tested to assess the contribution of adding the variables (Phedhazur & Schmelkin, 1991). All the variables were entered at the same time because there is no theoretical support for entering them in any specific order. Again, the sign and significance of each Beta were used to test the hypotheses (H6a, H6b, H7).

As was the case in phase 1 of Path I, the analysis was threatened by multicollinearity. Again, all VIFs were less than 10.

In phase 2 of the Path III analysis, the variables of interest were entered into a series of regression equations in a five-step process (Table 12). The change in $R^2$ was tested for significance to assess the contribution of adding the variables (Pedhazur & Schmelkin, 1991). In each step of the process, entrepreneurial intentions was the dependent variable. Age and level of education were the independent variables in step 1 and were used as control variables. The hierarchical regression procedure continued with the addition of breadth of past entrepreneurial, the positiveness of past entrepreneurial experience, and self-efficacy assessment (step 2), entrepreneurial self-efficacy (step 3), trigger event (step 4), and the interaction of trigger event and entrepreneurial self-efficacy (step 5). A significant change in $R^2$ for step 3 provides support for the association between entrepreneurial self-efficacy and entrepreneurial intentions (H5). A significant change in $R^2$ as the interaction term was entered (step 5), provides support for the moderating effect of a trigger event on the relationship between entrepreneurial self-efficacy and entrepreneurial intentions (part of H8).

### Results of the Path I Analysis

Hypotheses H2a and H2b suggested that the breadth and positiveness of past entrepreneurial experience are positively associated with the formation of perceived desirability of starting a business. Specifically, the more entrepreneurial experience a person has and the more positive he or she considers that experience, the more likely the individual is to view starting a business as desirable. Hypothesis H3 suggested that the degree of social support is positively associated with perceived desirability. That is, the more someone perceives that important others think he or she should start a business, the more desirable it is to start a business.

These hypotheses were tested in phase 1 of the Path I analysis using two steps. In step 1, the control variables of age and education were regressed on perceived desirability. As shown in Table 13, the $F$ of .40 was not significant indicating that age and level of education do not have a significant relation to perceived desirability. Next, social support, breadth of past entrepreneurial experience, and positiveness of past entrepreneurial experience were added to the previous equation (step 2). The model was significant ($F = 4.86$, df = 124, $p < .01$) and produced a significant change in $R^2$ ($\Delta R^2 = .162$, $p < .01$) (Table 13). Results provide support for the proposed positive relation between positiveness of past entrepreneurial experience and perceived desirability ($\beta = .25$, $p < .05$) (H2b). Results also supported the positive relationship between social support and perceived desirability ($\beta = .26$, $p < .01$) (H3). The hypothesized positive relation between breadth of past entrepreneurial experience and perceived desirability (H2a) was not supported ($\beta = .02$, $p > .05$). Overall, the results of phase 1 tests indicated that it is not the amount of past entrepreneurial experience, but how positive people view past experience and how supportive important others are to the notion of starting a business that are related to perceived desirability.

In phase 2 of the Path I analysis, a five-step series of regression equations were employed with entrepreneurial intentions as the dependent variable. These regression equations were used to test the hypothesized positive relation between perceived desirability and the formation of entrepreneurial intentions (H1) and the moderating effect of a trigger event on the perceived desirability-entrepreneurial intentions relationship (part of H8). In other words, it was expected that people who perceive entrepreneurship as desirable would form stronger intentions to start a business than those who did not. In addition, it was expected that the occurrence of a disrupting event (trigger event) in the normal pattern of a person's life would make the prospect of entrepreneurship more attractive and, thus, enhance the relationship between perceived desirability and the formation of entrepreneurial intentions.

Step 1 of the phase 2 analysis included age and level of education as independent variables and entrepreneurial intentions as the dependent variable. The results (Table 14) do not indicate that

**Table 13. Phase 1 of the Path I Analysis**

| Regression | Dependent Variable | Independent Variables | Beta | F | R² | ΔR² | Partial F |
|---|---|---|---|---|---|---|---|
| Step 1 | Perceived Desirability | | | .40 | .007 | .007 | .43 |
| | | Age | .04 | | | | |
| | | Education | -.08 | | | | |
| Step 2 | Perceived Desirability | | | 4.86** | .169 | .162 | 7.73** |
| | | [1]BPEE | .02 | | | | |
| | | [2]PPEE | .25* | | | | |
| | | [3]SS | .26** | | | | |

n = 125

[1]BPEE - Breadth of Past Entrepreneurial Experience

[2]PPEE - Positiveness of Past Entrepreneurial Experience

[3]SS - Social Support

* $p < .05$

** $p < .01$

**Table 14. Phase 2 of the Path I Analysis**

| Regression | Dependent Variable | Independent Variables | $F$ | $R^2$ | $\Delta R^2$ | Partial $F$ |
|---|---|---|---|---|---|---|
| Step 1 | Entrepreneurial Intentions | Age, Education | 1.74 | .028 | .028 | 1.76 |
| Step 2 | Entrepreneurial Intentions | [1]BPEE, [2]PPEE, [3]SS | 7.45** | .231 | .203 | 10.47** |
| Step 3 | Entrepreneurial Intentions | [4]PD | 15.77** | .445 | .214 | 45.50** |
| Step 4 | Entrepreneurial Intentions | [5]TE | 15.48** | .481 | .036 | 8.12** |
| Step 5 | Entrepreneurial Intentions | [6](TExPD) | 13.61** | .484 | .003 | .67 |

n = 125

[1] BPEE - Breadth of Past Entrepreneurial Experience

[2] PPEE - Positiveness of Past Entrepreneurial Experience

[3] SS - Social Support

[4] PD - Perceived Desirability

[5] TE - Trigger Event

[6] (TExPD) - Interaction of Trigger Event and Perceived Desirability

\* $p < .05$

\*\* $p < .01$

age and level of education are significantly related to entrepreneurial intentions ($F = 1.74$, df = 124, $p. > .05$). In step 2, breadth of past
entrepreneurial experience, positiveness of past entrepreneurial
experience, and social support were entered. This resulted in a significant change in $R^2$ ($\Delta R^2 = .203$, Partial $F = 31.41$, $p. < .01$). Perceived
desirability was added in step 3. The results supported the proposed
positive relationship between perceived desirability and entrepreneurial intentions ($\Delta R^2 = .214$, Partial $F = 45.5$, $p. < .01$) (H1).

Trigger event was added in step 4. The results indicated a sig-
nificant change in $R^2$ ($\Delta R^2 = .036$, Partial $F = 8.12$, $p. < .01$) (see Table
14). In step 5, the interaction of perceived desirability and trigger
event was added. The results did not support the proposed moderating impact of a trigger event on the perceived desirability-
entrepreneurial intentions relationship ($\Delta R^2 = .003$, Partial $F = .67$,
$p. > .05$) (part of H8).

In summary, the results of phase 2 of the path I analysis supported the concept that people who perceive entrepreneurship as
desirable form stronger intentions to start an enterprise. The results
did not support the moderating effect of a trigger event, but indicated
that a trigger may have a more direct impact on the formation of
intentions. This was indicated by the significant change in $R^2$
as the trigger event was added as an independent variable (step 4)
(see Table 14).

## Results of Path II Analysis

Hypothesis H4 suggested that a person's propensity for proactive
behavior was positively associated with the formation of entrepreneurial intentions. In addition, a portion of hypothesis H8 stated that
a trigger event would moderate and enhance the propensity for
proactive behavior-entrepreneurial intentions relationship. More
specifically, people who feel that they are relatively unconstrained
by situational forces and who work to change the environment
(propensity for proactive behavior) would form stronger entrepreneurial intentions than those who are not so predisposed. Also, it
was expected that the occurrence of a trigger event would enhance
the formation of entrepreneurial intentions for those people who
have a propensity for proactive behavior.

These hypotheses were tested in a four-step hierarchical regression procedure. First, age and level of education were entered into

an equation as independent variables and entrepreneurial intentions was used as the dependent variable (step 1). The results indicated that the model was not significant and that age and level of education were not related to entrepreneurial intentions ($F$ = 1.74, df = 124, $p.$ > .05) (see Table 15). In step 2, propensity for proactive behavior was entered. This resulted in a significant change in $R^2$ ($\Delta R^2$ = .076, Partial $F$ = 10.26, $p.$ < .01). The results provided support for the proposed positive association between propensity for proactive behavior and entrepreneurial intentions (H4). Trigger event was added in step 3. This resulted in a significant change in $R^2$ ($\Delta R^2$ = .089, Partial $F$ = 13.23, $p.$ < .01) (Table 15). Finally, the interaction of propensity for proactive behavior and a trigger event was added in step 4. This did not result in a significant change in $R^2$ ($\Delta R^2$ = .003, Partial $F$ = .44, $p.$ > .05) (Table 15). Therefore, the results did not support the proposed moderating effect of a trigger event on the propensity for proactive behavior-entrepreneurial intentions relationship (part of H8).

Overall, the results of the Path II analysis indicated that people who perceive that they are relatively unconstrained by situational forces and take action to change their environment form stronger intentions to start a business than those individuals who do not have such a propensity for proactive behavior. The occurrence of a trigger event does not appear to enhance the relationship between propensity for proactive behavior and the formation of entrepreneurial intentions, but may have a more direct impact on intentions formation as indicated by the significant change in $R^2$ ($\Delta R^2$ = .089, Partial $F$ = 13.23, $p.$ < .01) as the trigger event was added (step 3) (Table 15).

## Results of the Path III Analysis

Hypotheses H6a and H6b suggested that the breadth and positiveness of past entrepreneurial experience are positively associated with the formation of entrepreneurial self-efficacy. Specifically, the more entrepreneurial experience a person has and the more positively he or she perceives the past experience to be, the more likely that the person will believe that he or she is capable of starting a business. Hypothesis H7 posited that self-efficacy assessment was positively associated with the formation of entrepreneurial self-efficacy. That is, the more a person believes he or she has what it takes to start

**Table 15. Path II Analysis**

| Regression | Dependent Variable | Independent Variables | $F$ | $R^2$ | $\Delta R^2$ | Partial $F$ |
|---|---|---|---|---|---|---|
| Step 1 | Entrepreneurial Intentions | Age, Education | 1.74 | .028 | .028 | 1.76 |
| Step 2 | Entrepreneurial Intentions | [1]PPB | 4.68** | .104 | .076 | 10.26** |
| Step 3 | Entrepreneurial Intentions | [2]TE | 7.17** | .193 | .089 | 13.23** |
| Step 4 | Entrepreneurial Intentions | [3](TExPD) | 5.79** | .196 | .003 | .44 |

n = 125

[1]PPB - Propensity for Proactive Behavior

[2]TE - Trigger Event

[3]TExPD) - Interaction of Trigger Event and Perceived Desirability

\* $p < .05$

\*\* $p < .01$

a business (i.e., skills, ability, resources, etc.), the more that person would believe that he or she is capable of starting a business.

These hypotheses were tested in phase 1 of the Path III analysis using two steps. In step 1, age and level of education were entered as independent variables and entrepreneurial self-efficacy as the dependent variable. As shown in Table 16, the model was not significant ($F = 1.14$, df = 124, $p. > .05$) indicating that age and level of education do not have a significant relationship with entrepreneurial self-efficacy. The step 2 regression equation included breadth of past entrepreneurial experience, positiveness of past entrepreneurial experience, and self-efficacy assessment as additional independent variables. The model was significant ($F = 6.28$, df = 124, $p. < .01$) and produced a significant change in $R^2$ ($\Delta R^2 = .191$, Partial $F = 28.73$, $p. < .01$) (Table 16). Results provided support for the proposed positive relation between self-efficacy assessment and entrepreneurial self-efficacy ($\beta = .43$, $p. < .01$) (H7). The results did not support the proposed positive relationship between the positiveness of past entrepreneurial experience and entrepreneurial self-efficacy ($\beta = -.02$, $p. > .05$) (H6b). In addition, the results did not support the proposed positive relation between breadth of past entrepreneurial experience and entrepreneurial self-efficacy ($\beta = .08$, $p. > .05$) (H6a).

Overall, the results of the phase 1 tests indicate that people who believe they have what it takes to start a business believe that they are capable of successfully starting a business. The amount of perceived positiveness and breadth of past entrepreneurial experience, however, are not related to a person's overall assessment of his or her capability of starting a business.

In phase 2 of the Path III analysis, a five-step series of regression equations was used with entrepreneurial intentions as the dependent variable. These regression equations were used to test the hypothesized positive relationship between entrepreneurial self-efficacy and entrepreneurial intentions (H5) and the moderating effect of a trigger event on the entrepreneurial self-efficacy-entrepreneurial intentions relationship (part of H8). In other words, it was expected that people who think they are capable of starting a business would form intentions to start a business more often than those who do not think they are capable. In addition, it was expected that the occurrence of a trigger would enhance the formation of intentions for those who believe they are capable.

**Table 16. Phase 1 of the Path III Analysis**

| Regression | Dependent Variable | Independent Variables | Beta | $F$ | $R^2$ | $\Delta R^2$ | Partial $F$ |
|---|---|---|---|---|---|---|---|
| Step 1 | Entrepreneurial Self-Efficacy | | | 1.14 | .018 | .018 | 1.12 |
| | | Age | .09 | | | | |
| | | Education | .08 | | | | |
| Step 2 | Entrepreneurial Self-Efficacy | | | 6.28** | .209 | .191 | 9.58** |
| | | [1]PPEE | -.02 | | | | |
| | | [2]BPEE | .08 | | | | |
| | | [3]SEA | .43** | | | | |

$n = 125$

[1]PPEE - Positiveness of Past Entrepreneurial Experience

[2]BPEE - Breadth of Past Entrepreneurial Experience

[3]SEA - Self-Efficacy Assessment

\* $p < .05$

\*\* $p < .01$

Step 1 of the phase 2 analysis included age and level of education as the independent variables and entrepreneurial intentions as the dependent variable. The model was not significant indicating that age and level of education are not significantly related to entrepreneurial intentions ($F = 1.74$, df = 124, $P. > .05$) (Table 17). In step 2, breadth of past entrepreneurial experience, positiveness of past entrepreneurial experience, and self-efficacy assessment were added. This resulted in a significant change in $R^2$ ($\Delta R^2 = .381$, Partial $F = 76.72$, $p. < .01$) (Table 17). Entrepreneurial self-efficacy was entered in step 3. The results did not support the proposed positive relationship between entrepreneurial self-efficacy and entrepreneurial intentions ($\Delta R^2 = .011$, Partial $F = 2.23$, $p. > .05$) (H5).

Trigger event was added in step 4. The results indicated a significant change in $R^2$ ($\Delta R^2 = .019$, Partial $F = 3.96$, $p. < .05$) (see Table 17). In step 5, the interaction of entrepreneurial self-efficacy and trigger event was added. The change in $R^2$ of .01 was not significant (Table 17). The results did not support the proposed moderating effect of a trigger event on the entrepreneurial self-efficacy-entrepreneurial intentions relationship ($\Delta R^2 = .01$, Partial $F = 2.11$, $p. > .05$) (part of H8).

In summary, the results of phase 2 of the Path III analysis did not support the proposed positive relationship between a person's perceived capability of starting a business and the formation of intentions to start a business. In addition, the occurrence of a trigger event does not appear to enhance the relationship between entrepreneurial self-efficacy and the formation of entrepreneurial intentions, but may have a more direct impact on intentions as indicated by the significant change in $R^2$ as the trigger event was added as an independent variable (step 4) (see Table 17).

## CHAPTER SUMMARY

The findings from the data analysis were presented in this chapter. After presenting the correlations, descriptive statistics, and reliabilities for the variables included in the study, the results of the test of each hypothesis were reported.

Hypothesis 1 predicted that a person's perceived desirability of starting a business would be positively related to the formation of entrepreneurial intentions. This hypothesis was supported. Hypothesis 2b suggested that the positiveness of past entrepreneurial

**Table 17. Phase 2 of the Path III Analysis**

| Regression | Dependent Variable | Independent Variables | $F$ | $R^2$ | $\Delta R^2$ | Partial $F$ |
|---|---|---|---|---|---|---|
| Step 1 | Entrepreneurial Intentions | Age, Education | 1.74 | .028 | .028 | 1.76 |
| Step 2 | Entrepreneurial Intentions | [1]BPEE, [2]PPEE, [3]SEA | 16.48** | .409 | .381 | 25.57** |
| Step 3 | Entrepreneurial Intentions | [4]ESE | 14.26** | .420 | .011 | 2.23 |
| Step 4 | Entrepreneurial Intentions | [5]TE | 13.09** | .439 | .019 | 3.96* |
| Step 5 | Entrepreneurial Intentions | [6](TExESE) | 11.84** | .449 | .010 | 2.11 |

n = 125

[1]BPEE - Breadth of Past Entrepreneurial Experience

[2]PPEE - Positiveness of Past Entrepreneurial Experience

[3]SEA - Self-Efficacy Assessment

[4]ESE - Entrepreneurial Self-Effiacacy

[5]TE - Trigger Event

[6](TExESE) - Interaction of Trigger Event and Entrepreneurial Self-Efficacy

\* $p < .05$

\*\* $p < .01$

experience would be positively related to a person's perceived desirability of starting a business. This hypothesis also was supported. Hypothesis 3 suggesting that what important others think (social support) of his or her starting a business would be positively related to perceived desirability was supported. Support also was found for Hypothesis 4, which predicted that a propensity for proactive behavior would be positively associated with the formation of entrepreneurial intentions. Finally, hypothesis 7, which proposed that people who felt they had what it takes to start a business (self-efficacy assessment) would believe they could successfully start a business (entrepreneurial self-efficacy) was supported.

Hypotheses 2a, 5, 6a, 6b, and 8 were not supported. Hypothesis 2a predicted that the breadth of past entrepreneurial experience would be positively associated with a person's perceived desirability of starting a business. Hypothesis 5 suggested that entrepreneurial self-efficacy would be positively associated with the formation of entrepreneurial intentions. Hypotheses 6a and 6b proposed that both the breadth and positiveness of past entrepreneurial experience would be positively associated with a person's belief that he or she could start a business (entrepreneurial self-efficacy). Finally, hypothesis 8 predicted that the occurrence of a trigger event would moderate the three relationships between perceived desirability, the propensity for proactive behavior, and entrepreneurial self-efficacy and the formation of entrepreneurial intentions.

Chapter 5 will examine the results in depth and present possible modifications to the research model. In addition, both theoretical and practical implications will be presented followed by a discussion of the limitations of the current study. The chapter will conclude with suggestions for future research.

## CHAPTER V

# Discussion

This chapter presents an in-depth discussion of the results and implications of the current study. First, the findings for each of the hypotheses are reviewed with possible explanations why some of the expected relationships were not found. Next, implications of the findings for refining the research model are discussed. This is followed by a post hoc power analysis. The theoretical and practical implications of the study are then examined. Next, the limitations of the study are reviewed. Finally, directions for future research conclude this chapter.

## HYPOTHESIZED RELATIONSHIPS

### Hypothesis 1

Based on hypothesis 1, it was expected that the perceived desirability of starting a business would be positively associated with the formation of entrepreneurial intentions. That is, people who have a positive attitude toward starting a business and think that starting a business is a desirable behavior will likely form entrepreneurial intentions to do so. This relationship was supported in the study. The results of this study were consistent with prior research that investigated attitude toward a behavior and the formation of intentions (e.g., Doll & Ajzen, 1990; Schifter & Ajzen, 1985; Parker et al., 1990). In addition, two studies conducted by Krueger (1993) and Krueger and his associates (1995) that investigated the link between a similar measure of perceived desirability and the formation of entrepreneurial intentions produced results similar to the current study. Unlike the current study, which used a sample of individuals in the process of making a decision about a specific entrepreneurial behavior (i.e., becoming a real estate agent), the two studies by Krueger (1993) and Krueger et al., (1995) used a sample of university seniors who did not have specific entrepreneurial intentions. The consistency of results between this study, which focus on specific entrepreneurial intentions, and other studies, which focused on general entrepreneurial intentions, may provide additional support to Brockhaus's (1987) findings that a majority of entrepreneurs decide to start a business even before deciding what business to start. Overall, the support for hypothesis 1 indicates that the perceived desirability of entrepreneurship has a significant and positive relationship to the formation of entrepreneurial intentions.

## Hypotheses 2a, 2b, and 3

Another area of investigation of the current study was examination of three factors that may relate to the formation of perceived desirability. Hypotheses 2a and 2b proposed that the breadth (H2a) and positiveness (H2b) of past entrepreneurial experience would be positively related to the formation of favorable perceptions of perceived desirability. Hypothesis 3 predicted that the perceived desirability of entrepreneurship would be positively related to a person's perceptions of what important others think of the person engaging in entrepreneurial activity. That is, perceived desirability would be related to the amount of social support from important others such as friends, relatives, and mentors.

The results of the current study did not support the predicted relation between the breadth of past entrepreneurial experience and the formation of perceived desirability (H2a). The results, however, did confirm the positive relation between perceived desirability and positiveness of past entrepreneurial experience and the degree of social support (H2b and H3). Specifically, perceived desirability was not related to the quantity of past entrepreneurial experience, but was related to perceptions of how positive the past experience appeared to be and the degree of support from important others.

The results of the current study concerning breadth and positiveness of past entrepreneurial experience were consistent with findings of Krueger (1993). In Krueger's study, the amount of past entrepreneurial experience was not correlated with his measure of perceived desirability, but the positiveness of past experience was positively correlated. Again, unlike the current study that investigated the specific entrepreneurial behavior of becoming a real estate agent, Krueger investigated a general concept of entrepreneurial behavior. The findings of each study confirmed that individuals may form perceptions of desirability based on the quality of past experience and not the quantity. This appears to hold true for both perceptions of desirability for specific entrepreneurial behavior and for entrepreneurial behavior in general.

To provide a possible explanation why the breadth of past experience was not related to the attitude of perceived desirability, whereas the positiveness of past experience was related, the concept of attitude needs to be explored. Attitude (i.e., perceived desirability) is a learned predisposition to respond in a favorable or unfavorable manner toward something (i.e., entrepreneurship) (Fishbein & Ajzen, 1975). In addition, Ajzen and Fishbein (1980) posit that attitudes are a function of beliefs. That is, a person who believes that a behavior will have a positive outcome will hold a favorable attitude toward the behavior and a person who believes that the behavior will result in a negative outcome will hold an unfavorable attitude. Beliefs, in turn, are developed by evaluating past experiences (Ajzen & Fishbein, 1980). Therefore, it would be logical that developing a favorable attitude (i.e., perceived desirability) toward entrepreneurship would be based on favorable evaluation of past entrepreneurial experience (H2b).

The current study supported the predicted positive relationship between perceived desirability and social support (H3). More specifically, the current study found that the more support important others provided for the idea of starting a business, the more desirable the idea of starting a business became. This finding is consistent with the results of recent research (e.g., Carsurd, Gagillo, & Olm, 1987; Krueger, 1993; Scherer et al., 1989) that found exogenous variables, such as social support, have a direct effect on attitudes about a behavior.

## Hypothesis 4

Shapero's (1982) model of the entrepreneurial event suggested that it would be difficult to form intentions to start a business without a strong desire to take action on the intentions (Bagozze & Yi, 1989). In the current study, hypothesis 4 predicted that a person with a proactive personality (i.e., a propensity for proactive behavior) would be likely to form intentions to engage in entrepreneurship. That is, a person who feels unconstrained by situational and environmental forces and who is willing to seek opportunity, show initiative, take action, and persevere until closure (Bateman & Crant, 1993), is likely to form intentions to start a business. The findings of the current study support this hypothesis.

These findings are consistent with results from two other recent entrepreneurial studies. Crant (1996) found a positive relationship between a person with a proactive personality and his or her success as a real estate agent. Krueger (1993) found a positive relationship between Burger's (1985) "desirability of control" (a similar construct to propensity for proactive behavior) and the formation of entrepreneurial intentions. These two studies provide additional support for the results of the current study.

## Hypotheses 5, 6a, 6b, and 7

Hypothesis 5 predicted that entrepreneurial self-efficacy is positively associated with the formation of entrepreneurial intentions. Specifically, a person who believes that he or she can start a business is likely to form intentions to engage in entrepreneurship. The results of the current study did not support the predicted relationship. In fact, the results appear to be in contradiction to past research (e.g., Doll & Ajzen, 1990; Godin et al., 1990, Krueger, 1993; Krueger et al., 1995) that found a positive relation between measures of constructs similar to self-efficacy and the formation of entrepreneurial intentions. To develop a possible explanation for the contradictory findings of the current study, it is necessary to review the concept of self-efficacy and its measurement in more detail.

Self-efficacy is determined by asking respondents if they can perform at various levels of achievement for a specific task (Gist & Mitchell, 1992). Prior research, however, based on Ajzen's (1991) theory of planned behavior (e.g., Doll & Ajzen, 1900; Godin et al., 1990) and Shapero's (1982) model of the entrepreneurial event (e.g., Krueger, 1993; Krueger et al., 1995) used constructs such as perceived behavioral control (for Ajzen's model) and perceived feasibility (for Shapero's model) that are described as being like self-efficacy, but are not measured like self-efficacy. Each of these measures asks a variety of general questions about ability to perform a task and not about specific levels of achievement, which is required for self-efficacy measurement (Gist & Mitchell, 1992). For example, Krueger (1993) asked general questions such as, "Do you know enough to start a business?" and "How certain of success are you?" The current study, however, measured self-efficacy by asking for a yes/no response indicating if specific levels of real estate achievement (e.g., $500,000 in annual sales, $1,000,000 in annual sales, up to $10,000,000 in annual sales) could be accomplished. In addition, respondents were asked to rate how confident they were with their yes/no response (see Appendix, section 8). Overall, prior research tended to focus on general evaluations of activity while the current study focused on specific levels of activity, which is the focus of self-efficacy assessments.

Comparing the result of the current study to findings of prior research, it appears that people were able to form judgements about their ability to perform general levels of activity, but not judgements concerning specific levels of activity. As a result, prior research showed a positive relation between self-efficacy type measures and the formation of intentions, whereas the current research did not find such a relationship.

A possible speculation as to why this happened is that becoming a real estate agent was such a novel task to the respondents that they did not have enough information about becoming a real estate agent to form self-efficacy judgements about specific levels of activity. In other words, when asked about specific levels of real estate achievement required to develop a summary self-efficacy judgement, people had little knowledge of what was required to reach these levels of success. As a result, people who did not intend to become real estate agents may have thought: "I could do that." Also, it is possible that some people who did intend to become agents did not know what they could expect and thought: "I don't know if I can do that." As a result, self-efficacy judgements were not positively related to the formation of entrepreneurial intentions. Further research, however, would be needed to confirm this conjecture.

Hypothesis 6a and 6b suggested that the breadth and positiveness of past entrepreneurial experience would be positively associated with the formation of entrepreneurial self-efficacy. The current study did not support these relationships. Hypothesis 7 predicted a positive relationship between self-efficacy assessment and entrepreneurial self-efficacy. This relationship was supported.

To explain these findings, it is necessary to review the concept of self-efficacy formation. Recall that Gist and Mitchell (1992) suggest that self-efficacy is a summary judgement of a person's capability of performing a specific task. The self-efficacy judgement is formed by processing a variety of information cues through three types of individual assessments: attributional analysis of past experience, assessment of task requirements, and assessment of personal and situational resources/constraints. The breadth and positiveness of past entrepreneurial experience (hypotheses 6a, and 6b) were included to capture the attributional assessment of past experience. In addition, Gist and Mitchell (1992) suggested that for novel tasks, self-efficacy is primarily formed using the assessment of task requirements and the assessment of personal and situational constraints. The variable, self-efficacy assessment, was designed to capture both the assessment of the task requirements and the assessment of personal and situational constraints (hypothesis 7).

Extending Gist and Mitchell's (1992) theory to the current study, it would be reasonable that entrepreneurial self-efficacy would be formed primarily by the self-efficacy assessment because becoming a real estate agent was a novel entrepreneurial activity for the sample. Therefore, the formation of entrepreneurial self-efficacy would be positively related to a person's self-efficacy assessment (hypothesis 7), but not necessarily positively related to the breadth and positiveness of past entrepreneurial experience (hypotheses 6a and 6b). This is consistent with the findings of the current study.

Support for the positive relationship between self-efficacy assessment and entrepreneurial self-efficacy is still problematic for the overall research model because the relationship between entrepreneurial self-efficacy and the formation of entrepreneurial intentions was not supported. Post hoc analysis of the regression equations used to test the hypotheses revealed an interesting finding that may help solve the problem. While entrepreneurial self-efficacy was not positively related with the formation of intentions, self-efficacy assessment was. The Beta of .58 associated with self-efficacy assessment as one of the independent variables and entrepreneurial intentions as the dependent variable was significant ($p < .01$). In summary, entrepreneurial self-efficacy was not related to the formation of intentions, but self-efficacy assessment was.

To explain these findings, recall that respondents did not appear to be able to form self-efficacy judgements based on the specific levels of real estate activity because they were ignorant of what it took to perform at the various levels. Self-efficacy assessment, however, addresses specific tasks, abilities, skills, and resources needed to become a successful agent. As a result, this may imply that for a novel task, such as becoming a real estate agent, people may not have enough information to form a summary self-efficacy judgement based on specific levels of achievement where they do not understand what is required for them to successfully complete each level. When asked about specific tasks, skills, resources, etc., and their abilities (self-efficacy assessment), however, people were able to assess their own situation. Therefore, most respondents appeared better able to assess the specific details covered in the self-efficacy assessment and relate them to the formation of intentions. Thus, the results indicate that, for novel tasks, the self-efficacy assessment has a significant positive relationship to the formation of entrepreneurial intentions while self-efficacy does not.

**Hypothesis 8**

Hypothesis 8 predicted that a disruption in a person's life such as loss of a job, divorce, encouragement of a mentor, missed promotion, or birth of a child (i.e., a trigger event) would moderate the relationships between entrepreneurial intentions and perceived desirability, propensity for proactive behavior, and entrepreneurial self-efficacy. That is, the presence of a trigger event would strengthen these relationships. The results of this study did not support the predicted relationships.

Much of the research suggested that a trigger event often, but not always, encouraged changes in career (Osipow & Fitzgerald, 1996), even influencing the choice of entrepreneurship (Bacus and Human, 1994). Thus, the decision to become an entrepreneur could result from either a gradual change or a displacing event (Dyer, 1992; Gersick, 1991; Quinn, 1980; Van de Ven, 1992). This would imply that a trigger event has an enhancing effect on the decision to become an entrepreneur, but it is not a necessary condition.

A possible explanation why the current study did not support this reasoning may be found in research by Shapero (1975). In interviews with 109 entrepreneurs, he found that 93% of the respondents reported that either a positive or negative event impacted their decision to become an entrepreneur while only 7% did not report the influence of a trigger event. This could imply that a trigger event may have a more direct impact on a majority of the decisions to become an entrepreneur. Post hoc analysis of the data indicated that this may be the case. When a trigger event was added as an independent variable to each of the regression equations testing the relationship between entrepreneurial intentions and perceived desirability, propensity for proactive behavior, and entrepreneurial self-efficacy, there was a significant change in $R^2$ ($p. < .01$) (see step 4 in Table 12, step 3 in Table 13, and step 4 in Table 15). This would support a more direct relationship of a trigger event to the formation of entrepreneurial intentions. In other words, a trigger event was positively associated with the formation of entrepreneurial intentions, and did not function as a moderator.

Table 18 provides a summary of all the hypotheses tested in the current study. To confirm the study's findings, more research needs to be done in different entrepreneurial situations and with more refined measures. In different settings and with more refined measurement instruments, some of the hypotheses not supported in the current study may eventually find support.

### Implications for the Research Model

The findings suggest that several modifications should be made to the research model. Figure 7 presents the revised model showing the significant relationships found in the study. In the revised model, entrepreneurial intentions is positively associated with a trigger event, perceived desirability, propensity for proactive behavior, and self-efficacy assessment. Perceived desirability is positively associated with social support and positiveness of past entrepreneurial experience. Further research should be conducted to test and confirm the modifications to the research model.

### POST HOC POWER ANALYSIS

Prior to conducting the study, a power estimate was made using .80 as a standard for power (Cohen, 1988; Cohen & Cohen, 1983)

## Table 18. Summary of Hypotheses Tested

| Hypotheses | Support |
|---|---|
| H1: Perceived desirability is positively associated with the formation of entrepreneurial intentions. | S |
| H2a: The breadth of past entrepreneurial experience is positively associated with perceived desirability. | N |
| H2b: The positiveness of past entrepreneurial experience is positively associated with perceived desirability. | S |
| H3: Social support is positively associated with perceived desirability. | S |
| H4: A propensity for proactive behavior is positively associated with the formation of entrepreneurial intentions. | S |
| H5: Entrepreneurial self-efficacy is positively associated with the formation of entrepreneurial intentions. | N |
| H6a: The breadth of past entrepreneurial experience is positively associated with entrepreneurial self-efficacy. | N |
| H6b: The positiveness of past entrepreneurial experience is positively associated with entrepreneurial self-efficacy. | N |
| H7: Self-efficacy assessment is positively associated with entrepreneurial self-efficacy. | S |
| H8: The existence of a trigger event will moderate the relationships between perceived desirability, entrepreneurial self-efficacy, and propensity for proactive behavior and entrepreneurial intentions. That is, the presence of a trigger event will strengthen the relationships between perceived desirability, propensity for proactive behavior, and entrepreneurial self-efficacy, and entrepreneurial intentions. | N |

S = statistically significant support
N = not supported statistically

**Figure 7. Revised Model of Entrepreneurial Intentions**

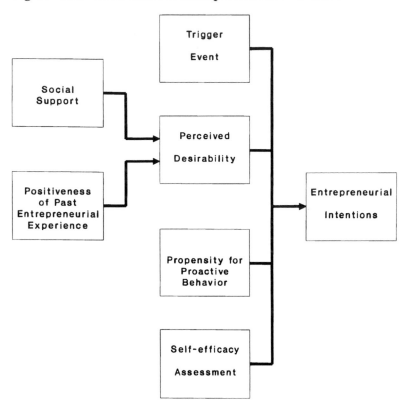

with an alpha of .05 and a projected medium effect size of .30 in the proposed relationships. A medium effect size was chosen because much entrepreneurial research provides results consisting of medium effect sizes (e.g., Crant, 1996; Krueger, 1993; Krueger et al., 1995). The analysis indicated that 136 respondents were necessary to detect a medium effect size. The useable number of questionnaires was 125.

Because a sample of 136 was necessary to detect a medium effect size, it was possible that the lack of support for hypotheses H2a, H5, H6a, H6b, and H8 was due to effects less than .30 that were not detected because of sample size. As a first check, a power analysis of the tests that supported hypotheses H1, H2b, H3, H4, and H7 was done. This analysis indicated that all tests had a power greater than .80 at an alpha of .05. The supporting tests meet or exceed the parameters suggested by Cohen (1988).

Hypothesis 8 had the most stringent sample requirements of all hypotheses in the study because there were a maximum of eight variables used in the regression equation, which is the most used in any of the tests. A power analysis was conducted using power of .80, an alpha of .05, and $n = 125$. The maximum effect size that could be detected under these conditions was $f^2 = .095$ [$f^2$ is the effect size index reported for multiple regression (Cohen, 1988)]. This indicates that a medium effect size could be detected (Cohen, 1988). As a result, if the effect sizes for the relationships in H2a, H5, H6a, H6b, and H8 were small ($f^2 < .01$), the current sample may not be capable of detecting them.

## IMPLICATIONS OF THE STUDY

The broad purpose of the current study was to be a theory-building effort in which the relationships among the personal traits and characteristics of the entrepreneur along with predisposing events were studied for their relation to the formation of entrepreneurial intentions. The study concentrated on Ajzen's (1991) theory of planned behavior and Shapero's (1982) model of the entrepreneurial event as the theoretical foundation for the study. By combining sound intentions-based models into one parsimonious research framework, the study provided greater understanding of the birth of a new firm. Because entrepreneurial activity is such a significant part of today's economy (Bygrave, 1993), a better understanding of the birth of business provided by the current study has important implications for theoretical investigations by researchers as well as practical applications by entrepreneurs, entrepreneurship educators, and policy makers.

### Theoretical Implications

A unique aspect of the current study was the use of a sample of individuals in which approximately half were in the process of deciding to become real estate agents. Unlike prior research that investigated the formation of entrepreneurial intentions in a general sense, this study used specific entrepreneurial activity. As a result, the findings of this study, which support the positive association between entrepreneurial intentions and perceived desirability and propensity for proactive behavior found in prior research (e.g., Crant, 1996; Krueger, 1993; Krueger et al., 1995), show that these relationships are significant for specific entrepreneurial activity as well as entrepreneurship in general. The findings suggest that perceived desirability and propensity for proactive behavior are both useful for research into general perceptions of entrepreneurial intentions and intentions to form specific business enterprises.

Results of the current study may provide additional insight into the formation of self-efficacy judgements for novel, specific entrepreneurial tasks. The results provide empirical support for Gist and Mitchell's (1992) theoretical proposition that for novel tasks, judgements of self-efficacy are formed primarily from the assessment of task requirements and perceptions of personal abilities and resource availability (i.e., self-efficacy assessment) and not from past experience. In addition, for novel tasks, it may be much easier for individuals to form entrepreneurial intentions from an examination of specific tasks, skills, abilities, and resources (i.e., self-efficacy assessment) required for successful task completion rather than a traditional summary judgement (i.e., entrepreneurial self-efficacy) based on specific levels of task achievement where they are ignorant of what is required.

Entrepreneurial research investigating the formation of entrepreneurial intentions could benefit from these findings. Because entrepreneurship is a novel task for many individuals, research should focus less on general summary self-efficacy judgements and more on the individual's assessment of his or her particular situation with regard to specific tasks, skills, abilities, and resources required to start a business.

Prior conceptual research (e.g., Bygrave, 1997; Martin, 1984; Shapero & Sokol, 1982), along with limited empirical research (e.g., Baucus & Human, 1994; Shapero, 1975), had suggested that a life disrupting event (i.e., trigger event) was important in the formation of entrepreneurial intentions. The current study provides additional empirical support for the importance of a trigger event. The findings suggest that a trigger event has more than a moderating effect on intentions formation; appears to be directly related to intentions formation. As a result, researchers should consider the effects of life disruptions to fully understand the entrepreneurial process.

Tests of Ajzen and Fishbein's (1980) theoretical proposition that intentions to behave in a certain way are directly influenced by what important others think of the behavior (i.e., social norm) has been mixed (Ajzen, 1991). More recent research has suggested that exogenous variables like social support, have a more direct relationship to attitudes about a behavior than the intentions to perform a behavior (Carsrud, Gagllio, & Olm, 1987; Krueger, 1993; Scherer et al., 1989). The current study provided support for the recent research. Social support had a significant positive relationship with perceptions of desirability, which in turn, was related to entrepreneurial intentions. As a result, researchers could capture the effects of exogenous variables such as social support, by assessing perceptions of desirability about forming a business. Since there are so many exogenous variables to consider, it is helpful to capture at least some of their effects in one construct.

Both the Ajzen (1991) model of planned behavior and the Shapero (1982) model of the entrepreneurial event suggest that past experience influences attitudes about specific behaviors. The current study provided empirical support for the relationship between positiveness of past experience and perceived desirability, but not the relationship between breadth of past experience and perceived desirability. That is, people tend to discount the quantity of past entrepreneurial experience and focus on perceptions of how positive the experience was. Consequently, entrepreneurship researchers may be able to concentrate only on the positive perceptions of past experience to fully understand the entrepreneurial process.

In summary, there are several benefits to entrepreneurial theory suggested by the current study and the revised model. Because many of the respondents used in this study were in the process of choosing the specific entrepreneurial activity of real estate, the positive relationships between the formation of intentions and perceived desirability and propensity for proactive behavior that were found in prior generic entrepreneurial intentions research were supported for specific entrepreneurial activity (i.e., real estate). For the novel task of starting a business, the formation of entrepreneurial intentions was found to be related to an assessment of specific tasks, skills, abilities, and resources needed to start a business rather than a general self-efficacy judgement. Perceptions of the desirability of entrepreneurship were positively related to the degree of social support and the evaluation of past entrepreneurial experience. Finally, life disrupting events (trigger events) were related to the formation of intentions.

## Practical Implications

Entrepreneurship is essential to the health of the United State's economy because small firms account for 38 percent of the gross domestic product and provide 40 to 80 percent of all new jobs (Dennis, 1993). The results of the current study provide practitioners such as entrepreneurs, entrepreneurship educators, and policy makers with a variety of practical implications that may aid in the development of vital entrepreneurial activity. By understanding how entrepreneurial intentions are formed, practitioners may be able to take advantage of the strong intentions-behavior relationship to foster new firm creation.

The results of the current study indicate that people who have a propensity for proactive behavior are more likely to form high entrepreneurial intentions than those who are not proactive. This would indicate that one way to detect potential entrepreneurs is to find individuals with a proactive personality.

One may question the practical implications of a simple personality measure to select potential entrepreneurs. This is a reasonable concern considering that past entrepreneurship research has concentrated primarily on traits (e.g., personality), and has had limited success in explaining the entrepreneurship process (Gartner, 1988). Gartner (1988) posits that what entrepreneurs do may explain more of the entrepreneurship process than who entrepreneurs are. Because propensity for proactive behavior links personality to potential behavior, it may provide the bridge between the two streams of research and thus, provide a useful predictive tool.

A major practical implication of the current study is that by knowing how intentions are formed, it may be possible to manipulate the process to encourage entrepreneurial behavior. For example, the results suggest that people who understand what it takes to achieve success and who positively evaluate their abilities, skills, and resources necessary for achievement (self-efficacy assessment) may form the intentions to start a business. The self-efficacy assessment could be enhanced by such actions as training in business skills (e.g., accounting, marketing, finance) or helping to develop a realistic business plan.

Another area with the potential to influence intentions is the perceived desirability of entrepreneurship. The current study suggests that social support and positiveness of past entrepreneurial experience relate to formation of perceptions of desirability. For example, by educating family and friends of potential entrepreneurs about the value of entrepreneurship, perceptions of desirability could be positively influenced. Establishing mentor or incubator programs would be an additional method for enhancing perceptions of desirability through positive social support.

The positiveness of past experience could be enhanced by providing positive exposure to entrepreneurship either through observation or direct contact. For example, individuals could be introduced to successful entrepreneurs who share their positive experiences. Potential entrepreneurs could be encouraged by providing intern programs so they could work directly with successful business people. These kinds of actions could enhance perceptions of desirability leading to the formation of entrepreneurial intentions.

The study's findings suggest that the opportunity for new firm creation is highest during times of life changing events. Corporate downsizing, plant relocation, plant closings, graduation from school, economic downturns, and family changes (e.g., birth of a child, death of a spouse, divorce) are all examples of trigger events that may be positively related to the formation of entrepreneurial intentions. During these disruptions, practitioners could cultivate entrepreneurship through the implementation of programs designed to enhance the formation of entrepreneurial intentions.

Overall, the potential to take advantage of the relationships that were supported in this study are many. Understanding how entrepreneurial intentions are formed could allow practitioners a vast array of opportunity to encourage entrepreneurial activity.

## LIMITATIONS OF THE STUDY

Because all information in the current study was collected from self-reports, the potential for common methods variance was great. Podsakoff and Organ (1986) suggest this is particularly true when two or more measures are taken from the same respondent (same source bias), as was the case in the current study. They also suggest that the most critical problem with self-reports is identifying the potential causes of artificial covariance between two variables that are supposedly distinct constructs. Artificial covariance could cause a correlation other than the underlying true relationship between the variables. As a result, findings of this type of study must be interpreted with caution.

Because of the nature of the current research study, data for the variables can be obtained only by the use of self-reports. All the variables in the study are measuring individual perceptions; therefore, the only way to collect the information is to ask the respondents. The current study is similar to other studies that have had to rely completely on self-reports for data collection (i.e., Crant, 1996; Krueger, 1993; Krueger et al., 1995).

Two procedural techniques suggested by Podsakoff and Organ (1986) were employed to help minimize the impact of common methods variance. First, measures contained in the questionnaire were constructed using different scaling techniques such as Likert scales, "yes"/"no" responses, and open-ended responses (see Appendix B). In addition, the scales were not arranged in any particular order. For example, the dependent variable (entrepreneurial intentions) is not the first variable, but is located in the middle of the questionnaire.

The second technique employed scale trimming (Podsakoff & Organ, 1986). Each scale was examined, and an attempt made to remove any duplicate questions. Other procedural remedies were not appropriate for this study. For example, Podsakoff and Organ (1986) suggested that data be collected at different times and in different settings. In the current study, the need for stability of measures precluded taking some of the measures at different times. There is too great a chance some event (e.g., rise in interest rates or a trigger event) could intervene in the time gap between collection periods and influence the perceptions of the respondents, thus, distorting the proposed relationships. In addition, it was not possible to administer the questionnaire more than once because a condition imposed by the cooperating school allowed only one visit.

As a check for the presence of same source bias, a post hoc analysis of the data was made using Harman's one factor test as suggested by Podsakoff and Organ (1986). This procedure requires that all variables of interest be entered into a factor analysis. The results of the unrotated factor solution are examined to determine the number of factors that are necessary to account for the variance in the variables. If either one factor emerges or one factor accounts for the majority of the covariance in the independent and dependent variables, common methods variance, or same source bias (the specific concern here) may be present (Podsakoff & Organ, 1986).

Results of the test on the data from the current study produced three factors with Eigenvalues greater that one. One principal factor, however, accounted for 34.7 percent of the variance while the other two factors accounted for 23.3 percent of the variance. In addition, most of the variables of interest loaded on the principal factor with loadings greater than .5. The results of the analysis suggest that same source bias may be a problem; therefore, interpretation of the results should be done with caution.

Two observations, however, may help provide more confidence in the study's results. First, some of the findings of the current study are consistent with past research. The significant positive relationship between propensity for proactive behavior and entrepreneurial intentions was consistent with research by Krueger, (1993) and Crant (1996) that used similar constructs. The significant positive relationships found in the current study between perceived desirability and intentions and between positiveness of past entrepreneurial experience and perceived desirability were consistent with research by Krueger (1993) and Krueger et al., (1995).

The second observation is that people in the sample were consistent in their perceptions. That is, people in the real estate portion of the sample and people in the non-real estate answered consistently. Those who were not interested in becoming an agent were consistent in their negative responses about becoming an agent just as those in the segment who wanted to be real estate agents were consistent in their positive responses. This indicates that people were answering according to their perceptions and not because of social desirability, a problem suggested by (Podsakoff & Organ, 1986).

Another potential limitation stems from the focus of the study on the act of becoming a real estate agent. In most cases, individuals who become agents will follow a prescribed process for building their business. Therefore, this entrepreneurial activity will not involve a high degree of innovation such as the development of new products, new processes, or new distribution systems. These kinds of activities are considered by many to be necessary for entrepreneurship (e.g., Bull & Willard, 1993; Schumpeter, 1936). Thus, there could be questions concerning the validity of applying the findings of this study to other forms of entrepreneurship because being a real estate agent does not satisfy some definitions of entrepreneurship.

It should be noted, however, that one of the primary strengths of the current study is that it does focus on individuals who are in the process of making a specific entrepreneurial decision. As mentioned previously, this addresses the problem in previous entrepreneurial research of including individuals in the sample who are not engaged in making an entrepreneurial decision. This approach to sampling brings the validity of the findings into question (Gartner, 1989). The selection of sample subjects who are in the decision process may help outweigh the questions of the proposed study's external validity just because becoming a real estate agent does not fit some definitions of entrepreneurship.

## DIRECTIONS FOR FUTURE RESEARCH

Future research could be directed down four different paths. First, there is opportunity to improve the current study and refine the research model. Second, additional research should be conducted that is directed at assessing the effect of manipulating the various variables that relate to the formation of intentions to either encourage or discourage entrepreneurial behavior. Third, the value of the current research depends on the strength of the intentions-behavior relationship. This relationship needs further study. Finally, research linking the research model to ultimate success of the business would be a long-term goal.

Several avenues of research could be employed to improve the current study and better improve the research model. A larger sample could be used to detect smaller effect sizes in some of the hypothesized relationships. Some of the concepts and measures could be refined to provide more specific information. For example, future research could focus on developing a self-efficacy assessment that could identify the specific skills, abilities, and resources that have the most impact on the formation of intentions. A more finely defined measure of the impact of the positiveness of past experience should be developed that would enable researchers to identify what kind of experiences have the greatest relationship to perceived desirability. Researchers might wish to examine whether what some specific, important others think provides more influence on perceived desirability than other sources of social support. Finally, future research could investigate the kinds of trigger events that have the most influence on the formation of intentions.

A persistent weakness of past entrepreneurship research has been the inability to select a sample of individuals serious about entrepreneurial activity who are in the process of making a decision about starting a business (Gartner, 1989). This study attempted to solve this weakness by selecting a sample in which some were actually in the process of making an entrepreneurial decision concerning becoming a real estate agent. Future research, however, needs to expand this type of study to include individuals considering entrepreneurial activity that requires innovation in areas such as products, processes, or distribution. Such innovations are often considered necessary for entrepreneurship.

Future researchers should investigate how the manipulation of the variables in the research model would impact the formation of entrepreneurial intentions. Researchers could determine if exposure to successful entrepreneurs, basic skills training, or development of social networks aids in raising the intentions to form a new business. In addition, researchers could determine if one type of manipulation has more impact than other types (e.g., Does skill training have more influence than social support?). The research opportunities along this avenue are almost limitless.

The value of the current research model is dependent on the strength of the intentions-behavior relationship. Entrepreneurial intentions have little use if they are not acted upon. Therefore, future research should more fully investigate this relationship. If a sample was used that contained individuals serious about entrepreneurship, then the subjects could be included in a longitudinal study to see whether they actually started the business they intended to start. A strong intentions-behavior relationship would help bridge the gap between the prestart-up phase and start-up phase in the business life cycle.

Finally, future research should investigate the relationship between the initial prestart-up conditions described in the research model and long-term firm success. For example, research questions such as, "Do individuals with a proactive personality have a better chance of success than others?" or "Does strong initial social support lead to firm success?" or "Do people who have a high self-efficacy assessment produce better long-term results?" would be important questions for further research. Again, the opportunity for future research along these lines is almost limitless.

## CHAPTER SUMMARY

The primary purpose of the study was to be a theory-building effort where the relationships among personal traits and characteristics of the entrepreneur along with predisposing events relate to the formation of entrepreneurial intentions. A research model based on Ajzen's (1991) theory of planned behavior and Shapero's (1982) model of the entrepreneurial event was developed with ten hypothesized relationships. This chapter begins with a discussion of the results of the ten proposed relationships.

Five of the ten relationships were supported. Perceived desirability was related to entrepreneurial intentions. Both the positiveness of past entrepreneurial experience and the amount of social support were positively related to the perceived desirability. A propensity for proactive behavior was related to the formation of entrepreneurial intentions. Finally, self-efficacy assessment was positively related to entrepreneurial self-efficacy.

The breadth of past entrepreneurial experience was not found to be related to perceived desirability. Entrepreneurial self-efficacy was not related to the formation of entrepreneurial intentions. Neither the breadth nor positiveness of past entrepreneurial experience were positively related to entrepreneurial self-efficacy. Finally, a trigger event was not found to moderate the relationship between entrepreneurial intentions and perceived desirability, propensity for proactive behavior, and entrepreneurial self-efficacy.

The discussion of the hypotheses was followed by implications for the research model. The primary implications were that a trigger event may have a direct impact on entrepreneurial intentions and for novel tasks, such as entrepreneurship, self-efficacy assessment may be positively related to intentions formation. This was followed by a power analysis that indicated that some of the non-supported relationships may be a result of insufficient sample size to detect small effect sizes.

Next, the chapter presented both theoretical and practical implications of the study. The following section discussed the limitations of the study with particular attention to the potential threat of common methods variance. The chapter concludes with a proposed research agenda to improve the current study and expand the scope of the current study to answer a variety of other research questions.

# Questionnaire

Introduction: I would appreciate your cooperation in a research project I am conducting about becoming a real estate agent. Please take your time to fill out this questionnaire as accurately as possible. All responses will be confidential.

**Section 1.**

**To what extent do you agree with the following statements. Please *circle* the appropriate number.**

1. I am constantly on the lookout for new ways to improve my life.
   strongly disagree ⌊1│2│3│4│5│6│7⌋ strongly agree
2. I feel driven to make a difference in my community, and maybe the world.
   strongly disagree ⌊1│2│3│4│5│6│7⌋ strongly agree
3. I tend to let others take the initiative to start new projects.
   strongly disagree ⌊1│2│3│4│5│6│7⌋ strongly agree
4. Wherever I have been, I have been a powerful force for constructive change.
   strongly disagree ⌊1│2│3│4│5│6│7⌋ strongly agree
5. I enjoy facing and overcoming obstacles to my ideas.
   strongly disagree ⌊1│2│3│4│5│6│7⌋ strongly agree
6. Nothing is more exciting than seeing my ideas turn into reality.
   strongly disagree ⌊1│2│3│4│5│6│7⌋ strongly agree
7. If I see something I don't like, I fix it.
   strongly disagree ⌊1│2│3│4│5│6│7⌋ strongly agree

8.  No matter what the odds, if I believe in something I will make it happen.
    strongly disagree ⌊1│2│3│4│5│6│7⌋ strongly agree
9.  I love being a champion for my ideas, even against others' opinions.
    strongly disagree ⌊1│2│3│4│5│6│7⌋ strongly agree
10. I excel at identifying opportunities.
    strongly disagree ⌊1│2│3│4│5│6│7⌋ strongly agree
11. I am always looking for better ways to do things.
    strongly disagree ⌊1│2│3│4│5│6│7⌋ strongly agree
12. If I believe in an idea, no obstacle will prevent me from making it happen.
    strongly disagree ⌊1│2│3│4│5│6│7⌋ strongly agree
13. I love to challenge the *status quo*.
    strongly disagree ⌊1│2│3│4│5│6│7⌋ strongly agree
14. When I have a problem, I tackle it head-on.
    strongly disagree ⌊1│2│3│4│5│6│7⌋ strongly agree
15. I am great at turning problems into opportunities.
    strongly disagree ⌊1│2│3│4│5│6│7⌋ strongly agree
16. I can spot a good opportunity long before others can.
    strongly disagree ⌊1│2│3│4│5│6│7⌋ strongly agree
17. If someone is in trouble, I help out in any way I can.
    strongly disagree ⌊1│2│3│4│5│6│7⌋ strongly agree

## Section 2.

**Please *circle* the appropriate number.**

1.  How would you feel if you became a real estate agent?
    I'd hate doing it ⌊1│2│3│4│5│6│7⌋ I'd love doing it
2.  How stressful would it be as a real estate agent?
    very stressful ⌊1│2│3│4│5│6│7⌋ not stressful at all
3.  How enthusiastic would you be as a real estate agent?
    not enthusiastic at all ⌊1│2│3│4│5│6│7⌋ very enthusiastic
4.  How much personal independence would you feel as a real estate agent?
    not independent at all ⌊1│2│3│4│5│6│7⌋ very independent
5.  How much personal satisfaction would you get as a real estate agent?
    not much at all ⌊1│2│3│4│5│6│7⌋ a great deal

## Section 3.

Please answer the following by *circling* either "yes" or "no" and then, *"if yes,"* using your best judgement, circle how "positive" or "negative" the experience was in the question that follows. *Be sure to circle "very negative," "negative," "neither positive or negative," "positive," or "very positive" if your first answer is "yes."*

1. Have your parents ever been real estate agents? yes no
   **If yes,** was their experience? (circle one)
   (very negative) (negative) (neither positive or negative)
   (positive) (very positive)

2. Do you know anyone else who is or has been a real estate agent? yes no
   **If yes,** was his or her experience? (circle one)
   (very negative) (negative) (neither positive or negative)
   (positive) (very positive)

3. Have you worked for any real estate company or agent? yes no
   **If yes,** was your experience? (circle one)
   (very negative) (negative) (neither positive or negative)
   (positive) (very positive)

4. Have you ever done any real estate activity (i.e., construction, owned rental property, etc.)? yes no **If yes,** was your experience? (circle one)
   (very negative) (negative) (neither positive or negative)
   (positive) (very positive)

5. Have your parents started a business other than real estate? yes no
   **If yes,** was their experience? (circle one)
   (very negative) (negative) (neither positive or negative)
   (positive) (very positive)

6. Do you know anyone else who has started a business other than real estate? yes no
   **If yes,** was his or her experience? (circle one)
   (very negative) (negative) (neither positive or negative)
   (positive) (very positive)

7. Have you ever worked for a small business other than real estate? yes no

**If yes,** was your experience? (circle one)
(very negative)  (negative)  (neither positive or negative)
(positive)  (very positive)
8.  Have you ever started you own business other than real estate?  **yes  no**
    **If yes,** was your experience? (circle one)
    (very negative)  (negative)  (neither positive or negative)
    (positive)  (very positive)

**Section 4.**

On a scale of 0% to 100% there is a _____% chance that I will take the Texas Real Estate License Exam in the near future.

**Section 5.**

**To what extent do you believe the following tasks and conditions are required for success as a real estate agent, and how would you assess *your* ability related to these factors or conditions? Please *circle* the number on the first scale that best indicates to what extent the factor or condition is important. Then, *circle* the number on the second scale describing *your* ability related to each of the factors or conditions..**

1.  Continually finding people to become buyers or sellers.
    not important $\lfloor 1 \mid 2 \mid 3 \mid 4 \mid 5 \mid 6 \mid 7 \rfloor$ very important
    How much ability do **you** have to continually find people to become buyers and sellers?
    very little $\lfloor 1 \mid 2 \mid 3 \mid 4 \mid 5 \mid 6 \mid 7 \rfloor$ more than enough
2.  Persuading people to buy or sell.
    not important $\lfloor 1 \mid 2 \mid 3 \mid 4 \mid 5 \mid 6 \mid 7 \rfloor$ very important
    How much ability do **you** have to persuade people to buy or sell?
    very little $\lfloor 1 \mid 2 \mid 3 \mid 4 \mid 5 \mid 6 \mid 7 \rfloor$ more than enough
3.  Helping buyers and sellers negotiate.
    not important $\lfloor 1 \mid 2 \mid 3 \mid 4 \mid 5 \mid 6 \mid 7 \rfloor$ very important
    How much ability do **you** have to help buyers and sellers negotiate?
    very little $\lfloor 1 \mid 2 \mid 3 \mid 4 \mid 5 \mid 6 \mid 7 \rfloor$ more than enough
4.  Handling the many details of several transactions at the same time.
    not important $\lfloor 1 \mid 2 \mid 3 \mid 4 \mid 5 \mid 6 \mid 7 \rfloor$ very important

How much ability do **you** have to handle the details of several transactions at the same time?

very little | 1 | 2 | 3 | 4 | 5 | 6 | 7 | more than enough

5. Maintaining regular contact with both buyers and sellers.

not important | 1 | 2 | 3 | 4 | 5 | 6 | 7 | very important

How much ability do **you** have to maintain regular contact with both buyers and sellers?

very little | 1 | 2 | 3 | 4 | 5 | 6 | 7 | more than enough

6. Solving problems related to real estate transactions.

not important | 1 | 2 | 3 | 4 | 5 | 6 | 7 | very important

How much ability do **you** have to solve problems related to real estate transactions?

very little | 1 | 2 | 3 | 4 | 5 | 6 | 7 | more than enough

7. Understanding changing market conditions to better identify customer wants and needs.

not important | 1 | 2 | 3 | 4 | 5 | 6 | 7 | very important

How much ability do **you** have to understand changing market conditions?

very little | 1 | 2 | 3 | 4 | 5 | 6 | 7 | more than enough

8. Helping arrange financing.

not important | 1 | 2 | 3 | 4 | 5 | 6 | 7 | very important

How much ability do **you** have to help arrange financing?

very little | 1 | 2 | 3 | 4 | 5 | 6 | 7 | more than enough

9. Managing your time to meet the demands of both buyers and sellers.

not important | 1 | 2 | 3 | 4 | 5 | 6 | 7 | very important

How much ability do **you** have to manage your time to meet the demands of buyers and sellers?

very little | 1 | 2 | 3 | 4 | 5 | 6 | 7 | more than enough

10. Having sufficient time to become a real estate agent.

not important | 1 | 2 | 3 | 4 | 5 | 6 | 7 | very important

How much time do **you** have to become a real estate agent?

not enough | 1 | 2 | 3 | 4 | 5 | 6 | 7 | more than enough

11. Having sufficient money to become a real estate agent.

not important | 1 | 2 | 3 | 4 | 5 | 6 | 7 | very important

How much money do **you** have to become a real estate agent?

not enough | 1 | 2 | 3 | 4 | 5 | 6 | 7 | more than enough

12. Having support (i.e., encouragement, financial, etc.) from family and friends to become a real estate agent.

not important | 1 | 2 | 3 | 4 | 5 | 6 | 7 | very important

How much support do **you** have to become a real estate agent?

not enough ⌊1│2│3│4│5│6│7⌋ more than enough

13. Having the physical energy to do the work required to become a real estate agent.

not important ⌊1│2│3│4│5│6│7⌋ very important

How much physical energy do **you** have to do the work to become an agent?

not enough ⌊1│2│3│4│5│6│7⌋ more than enough

14. Having a local economy healthy enough to become a successful agent.

not important ⌊1│2│3│4│5│6│7⌋ very important

Is the local economy healthy enough for **you** to be successful?

not enough ⌊1│2│3│4│5│6│7⌋ more than enough

15. Having adequate self-motivation.

not important ⌊1│2│3│4│5│6│7⌋ very important

Are **you** self-motivated enough to be a successful agent?

not enough ⌊1│2│3│4│5│6│7⌋ more than enough

**Section 6.**

**Please answer the following by *circling* the number or term that best describes how you feel.**

1a. If I were considering becoming a real estate agent, my family would think that

I should ⌊1│2│3│4│5│6│7⌋ I should **not** become a real estate agent.

1b. In general, how much would you want to do what your family thinks? (circle one)

**not at all     slightly     moderately     strongly**

2a. If I were considering becoming a real estate agent, my friends would think that

I should ⌊1│2│3│4│5│6│7⌋ I should **not** become a real estate agent.

2b. In general, how much would you want to do what your friends thinks? (circle one)

**not at all     slightly     moderately     strongly**

**Section 7.**

Please answer the following by *circling* either "yes" or "no." If "yes," please indicate the degree of influence these events have had on your life by *circling* (not at all), (slightly), (moderately), or (strongly).

1. Have there been any recent changes in your life situation? (for example, marriage or divorce, the birth or loss of a child, graduation, move to a new city) **yes   no**
1b. **If yes,** how much have these changes influenced your life?
   **not at all     slightly     moderately     strongly**
2. Have there been any recent changes in your work situation? (for example, promotion, loss of job, missed promotion, raise, missed raise) **yes   no**
2b **If yes,** how much have these changes influenced your life?
   **not at all     slightly     moderately     strongly**
3. Have you recently changed your assessment of your career prospects? (for example, better opportunity available, less opportunity available, desire for a career change) **yes   no**
3b. **If yes,** how much have these assessments influenced your life?
   **not at all     slightly     moderately     strongly**
4. Has anyone in the real estate business encouraged you to become a real estate agent? **yes   no**
4b. **If yes,** how much has this person influenced your life?
   **not at all     slightly     moderately     strongly**


**Section 8.**

Please *circle* a yes or no answer to each statement. Then record your *certainty* of your yes/no answer on the adjoining line using a scale of 0% to 100%.

**Example:**   I can pass the Texas real estate license exam.
         **Yes   No**__97%__ % certainty

(This would indicate that you are 97% certain that you **can** pass the exam. If you had circled **"no,"** this would indicate that you are 97% certain that you **cannot** pass the exam.)

1. I could produce $500,000 in sales my first year in a real estate business. [Approximately one average-priced house ($85,000) every other month.]
   **Yes No** _____ % certainty
2. I could produce $1,000,000 in sales my first year in a real estate business. [Approximately one average-priced house ($85,000) every month]
   **Yes No** _____ % certainty
3. I could produce $2,000,000 in sales my first year in a real estate business. [Approximately two average-priced houses ($85,000) every month.]
   **Yes No** _____ % certainty
4. I could produce $3,000,000 in sales my first year in a real estate business. [Approximately three average-priced houses ($85,000) every month.]
   **Yes No** _____ % certainty
5. I could produce $4,000,000 in sales my first year in a real estate business. [Approximately four average-priced houses ($85,000) every month.]
   **Yes No** _____ % certainty
6. I could produce $5,000,000 in sales my first year in a real estate business. [Approximately five average-priced houses ($85,000) every month.]
   **Yes No** _____ % certainty
7. I could produce $10,000,000 in sales my first year in a real estate business. [Approximately ten average-priced houses ($85,000) every month.]
   **Yes No** _____ % certainty

**Note: Be sure that you have marked a *certainty* for *all* responses, both "yes" and "no."**

**Please provide additional information about yourself.**

Sex     M \_\_\_\_\_     F \_\_\_\_\_          Age \_\_\_\_\_

Please indicate the amount of formal education you have. Please place an **X** by the appropriate response.

\_\_\_\_\_ Less than high school
\_\_\_\_\_ High school graduate

_____ Some college
_____ Completion of a two-year degree
_____ Completion of a four-year degree
_____ Completion of a masters degree
_____ Completion of a Ph.D.

How many years of full-time (40 hrs./week or more) work experience have you had? _____ years

Are you taking the class for semester hour credit or continuing education credit? Please **circle** the appropriate response.

**Semester hour     Continuing education**

If you do not intend to become a real estate agent, do you intend to start any kind of business in the near future?   **yes   no**

**I would like to follow-up with you in the near future (3 to 4 months). If you will volunteer for a follow-up please provide the following:**

Name:_____
Address:_____
Phone number: (_____) _____-_____

**Thank You**

# References

Ajzen, I. (1985). From intentions to actions: A theory of planned behavior. In J. Kuhl & J. Beckmann (Eds.) *Action-control: From cognition to behavior* (pp. 11–39). Heidelberg: Springer.

Ajzen, I. (1987). Attitudes, traits, and actions: Dispositional prediction of behavior in personality and social psychology. In L. Berkowitz (Ed.) *Advances in experimental social psychology* (vol. 20. pp. 1–63). New York: Academic Press.

Ajzen, I. (1991). The theory of planned behavior. *Organizational Behavior and Human Decision Processes, 50,* 179–211.

Ajzen, I, & Fishbein, M. (1980). *Understanding attitudes and predicting social behavior.* Englewood Cliffs, NJ: Prentice-Hall.

Ajzen, I., & Madden, T. L. (1986). Prediction of goal-directed behavior: Attitudes, intentions, and perceived behavioral control. *Journal of Experimental Social Psychology, 22,* 453–474.

Bagozzi, R. & Yi, Y. (1989). The degree of intention formation as a moderator of the attitude-behavior relationship. *Social Psychology Quarterly, 52,* 266–279.

Bandura, A. (1977). *Social learning theory.* Englewood Cliffs, NJ: Prentice Hall.

Bandura, A. (1982). Self-efficacy mechanism in human agency. *American Psychologist, 37,* 122–147.

Bandura, A. (1986). *Social foundations of thought and action: A social-cognitive view.* Englewood Cliffs, NJ: Prentice-Hall.

Bandura, A. (1988). Organizational applications of social cognitive theory. *Australian Journal of management, 13,* 137–164.

Bandura, A., & Wood, R. E. (1989). Effect of perceived controllability and performance standards on self-regulation of complex decision making. *Journal of Personality and Social Psychology, 56,* 805–814.

*119*

Barling, J., & Beattie, R. (1983). Self-efficacy beliefs and sales performance. *Journal of Organizational Behavior Management, 5,* 41–51.

Bateman, T. S., & Crant, J. M. (1993). The proactive component of organizational behavior: A measure and correlates. *Journal of Organizational Behavior, 14,* 103–118.

Baucus, D. A., Human, S. E. (1994). Second-career entrepreneurs: A multiple case study analysis of entrepreneurial processes and antecedent variables. *Entrepreneurship Theory and Practice, 19*(2), 41–71.

Beal, D. A., & Manstead, A. S. R. (1991). Predicting mothers' intentions to limit frequency of infants' sugar intake: Testing the theory of planned behavior. *Journal of Applied Social Psychology, 21,* 409–431.

Behave, M. P. (1994). A process model of entrepreneurial venture creation. *Journal of Business Venturing, 9,* 223–242.

Bird, B. (1988). Implementing entrepreneurial ideas: The case for intentions. *Academy of Management Review, 13,* 442–453.

Bird, B. J. (1989). *Entrepreneurial behavior.* Glenview, IL: Scott, Foresman, and Company.

Bird, B. J. (1992). The operation of intentions in time: The emergence of the new venture. *Entrepreneurship Theory and Practice, 17*(1), 11–20.

Bird, B., & Jelinek, M. (1988). The operation of entrepreneurial intentions. *Entrepreneurship Theory and Practice, 13*(2), 21–29.

Bonifay, P. H., Eon, J. F., Labre, H., & Meler, J. *La Creation D'Enterprise.* Doctoral Dissertation, The University of Texas at Austin.

Boswell, J. (1972). *The rise and decline of small firms.* London: George Allen and Unwin.

Boyd, N. G., & Vozikis, G. S. (1994). The influence of self-efficacy on the development of entrepreneurial intentions and actions. *Entrepreneurship Theory and Practice, 18*(4), 63–77.

Breckler, S. J. (1984). Empirical validation of affect, behavior, and cognition as distinct components of attitude. *Journal of Personality and Social Psychology, 47,* 1191–1205.

Brenner, O. C., Pringle, C. D., Greehaus, J. H. (1991). Perceived fulfillment of organizational employment versus entrepreneurship: Work values and career intentions of business college graduates. *Journal of Small Business Management, 29*(3), 62–74.

Brockhaus, R. H. (1980). Risk taking propensity of entrepreneurs. *Academy of Management Journal, 23,* 509–520.

Brockhaus, R. H. (1982). The psychology of the entrepreneur. In C. A. Kent, D. L. Sexton, & K. H. Vesper (Eds.), *Encyclopedia of entrepreneurship* (pp. 25–48). Englewood Cliffs, NJ: Prentice-Hall.

Brockhaus, R. H., & Horwitz, P. S. (1986). The psychology of the entrepreneur. In D. L. Sexton, & R. W. Smilor (Eds.), *The art and science of entrepreneurship* (pp. 25–60). Cambridge, MA: Ballinger Publishing Co.

Brockner, B., 1988. *Self-esteem at work.* Lexington, MA: Lexington Books.

Bull, I., & Willard, G. E. (1993). Towards a theory of entrepreneurship. *Journal of Business Venturing, 8,* 183–195.

Buss, A., & Finn, S. (1987). Classification of personality traits. *Journal of Personality and Social Psychology, 52,* 432–444.

Bygrave, W. D. (1989). The entrepreneurship paradigm (II): Chaos and catastrophes among quantum jumps. *Entrepreneurship Theory and Practice, 14*(2), 7–30.

Bygrave, W. D. (1993). Theory building in the entrepreneurial paradigm. *Journal of Business Venturing, 23,* 255–280.

Bygrave, W. D. (1997). The entrepreneurial process. In W. D. Bygrave (Ed.) *The portable MBA in entrepreneurship* (2nd ed.) (pp. 1–26). New York: John Wiley & Sons, Inc.

Carland, J. W., Hoy, F., & Carland J. A. C. (1988). "Who is an entrepreneur?" Is a question worth asking. *American Journal of Small Business, 12,* 33–40.

Carroll, J. H. (1965). *The Filipino manufacturing entrepreneur.* Ithaca, NY: Cornell University.

Carsrud, A., Gaglio, C., & Olm, K. (1987). Entrepreneurs-mentors, networks, and successful new venture development. *American Journal of Small Business, 12*(2), 13–18.

Carsrud, A. L., & Krueger, N. F. Jr. (1995). Entrepreneurship and social psychology: Behavioral technology for understanding the new venture initiation process. *Advances in Entrepreneurship, Firm Emergence, and Growth, 2,* 73–96.

Cohen, J. (1988). *Statistical power analysis for the behavioral sciences* (2nd ed.). Hillsdale, NJ: Lawrence Erlbaum Associates.

Cohen, J., & Cohen, P. (1983). *Applied multiple regression/correlation analysis for the behavioral sciences.* Hillsdale, NJ: Lawrence Erlbaum Associates, Publishers.

Crant, J. M. (1996). The proactive personality scale as a predictor of entrepreneurial intentions. *Journal of Small Business Management, 34*(3), 42–49.

Dennis, W. J. (1993). A small business primer: Charts and graphs illustrating the importance and role of American small business. *NFIB Quarterly Report for Small Business,* Aug., 1–49.

Doll, J., & Ajzen, I. (1990). *The effects of direct experience on the attitude-behavior relation: Stability versus accessibility.* Unpublished manuscript, Psychologisches Institut I, Universitat Hamburg, West Germany.

Dyer, G. (1992). *The entrepreneurial experience.* San Francisco, CA: Josey-Bass.

Gartner, W. B. (1985). A conceptual framework for describing the phenomenon of new venture creation. *Academy of Management Review, 10,* 696–706.

Gartner, W. B. (1988). "Who is an entrepreneur?" Is the wrong question. *American Journal of Small Business, 12,* 11–32.

Gartner, W. B. (1989). Some suggestions for research on entrepreneurial traits and characteristics. *Entrepreneurship Theory and Practice, 14,* 27–37.

Gatewood, J. E., Shaver, K. G., & Gartner, W. B. (1995). A longitudinal study of cognitive factors influencing start-up behaviors and success at venture creation. *Journal of Business Venturing, 10,* 371–391.

Gersick, C. J. G. (1991). Revolutionary change theories: A multilevel exploration of the punctuated equilibrium paradigm. *Academy of Management Review, 16,* 10–36.

Gist, M. E. (1987). Self-efficacy: Implications for organizational behavior and human resource management. *Academy of Management Review, 12,* 472–485.

Gist, M. E., & Mitchell, T. R. (1992). Self-efficacy: A theoretical analysis of its determinants and malleability. *Academy of Management Review, 17,* 183–211.

Godin, G., Valois, P. Jobin, J., & Ross, A. (1990). *Prediction of intention to exercise of individuals who have suffered from coronary heart disease.* Unpublished manuscript, School of Nursing, Laval University, Quebeck, Canada.

Herbert, R. F., & Link, A. N. (1982). *The entrepreneur: Mainstream views and radical critiques.* New York: Praeger.

Hill, T., Smith, N. D., & Mann, M. F. (1987). Role of efficacy expectations in predicting the decision to use advanced technology. *Journal of Applied Psychology, 72,* 307–314.

Hisrich, R., & Brush, C. (1984). The woman entrepreneur: Management skills and business problems. *Journal of Small Business Management, 22*(1), 31–37.

Holmes, T., & Cartwright, S. (1993). Career change: Myth or reality? *Employee Relations, 15*(6), 37–53.

Katz, J., & Gartner, W. B. (1988). Properties of emerging organizations. *Academy of Management Review, 13,* 429–441.

Kim, M. S., & Hunter, J. (1993). Relationships among attitude, behavioral intentions, and behavior. *Communication Research, 20,* 331–364.

Krech, D., Crutchfield, R. S., & Ballacher, E. L. (1962). *Individual in society.* New York: McGraw-Hill.

Krueger, N. F. Jr. (1989). Antecedents of opportunity recognition: The role of perceived self-efficacy. (Doctoral dissertation, The Ohio State University, 1989). Ann Arbor, MI: UMI Dissertation Services.

Krueger, N. F. Jr. (1993). The impact of prior entrepreneurial exposure on perceptions of new venture feasibility and desirability. *Entrepreneurship Theory and Practice, 18*(1), 5–21.

Krueger, N. F. Jr., & Brazeal, D. V. (1994). Entrepreneurial potential and potential entrepreneurs. *Entrepreneurship Theory and Practice, 18*(3), 91–104.

Krueger, N. F. Jr., Reilly, M. D., & Carsrud, A. L. (1995). *Entrepreneurial intentions: A competing models Approach.* Paper presented at the United States Association of Small business and Entrepreneurship, Boulder, CO.

Langer, E. (1983). *The psychology of control.* Beverly Hills, CA: Sage.

Latvak, I. A., & Maule, C. J. (1971). *Canadian entrepreneurship: A study of small newly established firms.* Ottawa, Canada: Department of Industry, Trade, and Commerce.

Learned, K. E. (1992). What happened before the organization? A model of organization formation. *Entrepreneurship Theory and Practice, 17*(1), 39–48.

LePiere, R. T. (1934). Attitudes and action. *Social Forces, 13*, 230–237.

Leavitt, H. (1988). *Managerial psychology: Managing behavior in organizations.* Chicago, IL: Dorsey Press.

Lee, C., & Bobko, P. (1994). Self-efficacy beliefs: Comparison of five measures. *Journal of Applied Psychology, 79*, 364–369.

Lent, R. W., Brown, S. D., & Larkin, K. C. (1987). Comparison of three theoretical derived variables in predicting career and academic behavior: Self-efficacy, interest congruence, and consequence thinking. *Journal of Counseling Psychology, 69*, 293–298.

Levinson, D. J. (1978). *The seasons of a man's life.* New York: Knopf.

Locke, E. A., Frederick, E., Lee, C., & Bobko, P. (1984). Effect of self-efficacy, goals, and task strategies on task performance. *Journal of Applied Psychology, 69*, 241–251.

Low, M. B., & MacMillian, I. C. (1988). Entrepreneurship: Past research and future challenges. *Journal of Management, 14*, 139–161.

MacMillian, I. C., & Katz, J. A. (1992). Idiosyncratic milieus of entrepreneurial research: The need for comprehensive theories. *Journal of Business Venturing, 7*, 1–8.

Martin, M. J. C. (1984). *Managing technological innovation and entrepreneurship*. Reston, VA: Reston Publishing.

Matthews, D. H., & Moser, S. B. (1996). A longitudinal investigation of the impact of family background and gender on interest in small firm ownership. *Journal of Small Business Management, 34*(2), 29–43.

McClelland, D. C. (1961). *The achieving society*. Princeton, NJ: Van Nostrand.

Mendenhall, W., & Sincich, T. (1989). *A second course in business statistics: Regression Analysis* (3rd ed.). San Francisco, CA: Dellen Publishing Company.

Moore, C. (1986). Understanding entrepreneurial behavior. In J. A. Pierce II, & R. B. Robinson Jr. (Eds.) *Academy of Management Best Papers Proceedings*, Chicago IL: Academy of Management.

Naffziger, D. W., Hornsby, J. S., & Kuratko, D. F. (1994). A proposed model of entrepreneurial motivation. *Entrepreneurship Theory and Practice, 18*(3), 29–42.

Nance, C. P. (1996). *Modern real estate practices in Texas* (8th ed.). Chicago, IL: Real Estate Education Company.

Netemyer, R. G., Andrews, J. C., & Durvasala, S. (1990). *A comparison of three behavioral intention models using within and across subjects design*. Unpublished manuscript, Marketing Department, Louisiana State University at Baton Rouge.

Neter, J., Wasserman, W., Kunter, M. H. (1990) *Applied linear statistical models* (3rd ed.). Homewood, IL: Irwin.

Osipow, S. H., & Fitzgerald, L. F. (1996). *Theories of career development* (4th ed.). Boston, MA: Allyn and Bacon.

Parker, D., Manstead, A. S. T., Stradling, S. G., Reason, F. T., & Baxter, J. S. (1990). *Intention to commit driving violations: An application of the theory of planned behavior*. Unpublished manuscript, Department of Psychology, University of Manchester, Manchester, England.

Pedhazur, E. J., & Schmelkin, L. P. (1991). *Measurement, design, and analysis*. Hillsdale, NJ: Lawrence Erlbaum Associates, Publishers.

Podsakoff, P. M., & Organ, D. W. (1986). Self-reports in organizational research: Problems and prospects. *Journal of Management, 12*, 531–544.

Quinn, J. (1980). *Strategies for change: Logical incrementalism*. Homewood, IL: Irwin.

Reynolds, P. D. (1992). Sociology and entrepreneurship: Concepts and contributions. *Entrepreneurship Theory and Practice, 16*(2), 47–70.

Rosenberg, M. J., & Hovland, C. I. (1960). Cognitive, affective, and behavioral components of attitudes. In C. I. Hovland, & M. J. Rosenberg

(Eds.) *Attitude organization and change* (pp. 1–14). New Haven CT: Yale University Press.

Rotter, J. B. (1966). *Generalized expectancies for internal versus external control of reinforcement.* Washington D. C. The American Psychological Association.

Schere, J. (1982). Tolerance for ambiguity as a discriminating variable between entrepreneurs and managers. *Proceedings* (pp. 404–408). New York: Academy of Management.

Scherer, R., Adams, J., Carley, S., & Wiebe (1989). Role model performance effects on development of entrepreneurial career performance. *Entrepreneurship Theory and Practice, 13,* 53–81.

Schifter, D. B., & Ajzen, I. (1985). Intention, perceived control, and weight loss: An application of the theory of planned behavior. *Journal of Personality and Social Psychology, 49,* 843–851.

Schlegel, R. P., d'Averna, J. R., DeCourville, N. H., & Manske, S. R. (1990). *Problem drinking: A problem for the theory of reasoned action?* Unpublished manuscript. Department of Health Studies, University of Waterloo, Waterloo, Canada.

Schneider, B. (1983). Interactional psychology and organizational behavior. In L. Cummings, & B. Staw (Eds.). *Research in organizational behavior* vol. 5 (pp. 1–31). Greenwich, CT: JAI Press.

Schumpeter, J. A. (1936). *The theory of economic development* (2nd ed.). Cambridge, MA: Harvard University Press.

Shapero, A. (1975). The displaced, uncomfortable entrepreneur. *Psychology Today,* (November), 83–133.

Shapero, A. (1982). Social dimensions of entrepreneurship. In C. A. Kent, D. L. Sexton, & K. H. Vesper (Eds.) *Encyclopedia of entrepreneurship* (pp. 72–90). Englewood Cliffs, NJ: Prentice-Hall.

Shapero, A., & Sokol, L. (1982). The social dimensions of entrepreneurship. In C. A. Kent, D. L. Sexton, & Vesper, K. H. (Eds.). *Encyclopedia of entrepreneurship* (pp. 72–90). Englewood Cliffs, NJ: Prentice-Hall.

Shaver, K., & Scott, L. (1992). Person, process, choice: The psychology of new venture creation. *Entrepreneurship Theory and Practice, 16*(2), 23–45.

Sheppard, B., Hartwick, J., & Warshaw (1988). The theory of reasoned action: A meta-analysis of past research with recommendations for future research. *Journal of Consumer Research, 15,* 325–344.

Stumpf, S. A., Brief, A. P., & Hartman (1987). Self-efficacy expectations and coping with career-related events. *Journal of Vocational behavior, 31,* 91–108.

Taylor, M. S., Locke, E. A., Lee, C., & Gist, M. E. (1984). Type A behavior and faculty research productivity: What are the mechanisms? *Organizational Behavior and Human Decision Processes, 34,* 402–418.

Tushman, M., & Romanelli, E. (1985). Organizational evolution: A metamorphosis model of convergence and reorientation. In L. L. Cummings & B. M. Staw (Eds.). *Research in organizational behavior* vol. 7 (pp. 171–222). Greenwich, CT: JAI Press.

van Ryn, M., & Vinokur, A. D. (1990). *The role of experimentally manipulated self-efficacy in determining job-search behavior among the unemployed.* Unpublished manuscript, Institute for Social Research, University of Michigan at Ann Arbor.

Van de Ven, A. (1992). Suggestions for studying strategy process. *Strategic Management Journal, 13,* 169–188.

Vesper, K. H. (1980). *New venture strategies.* Englewood Cliffs, NJ: Prentice-Hall.

Vesper, K. H. (1990). *New venture strategies* (rev. ed.). Englewood Cliffs, NJ: Prentice-Hall.

Vroom, V. H. (1964). *Work and motivation.* New York: Wiley.

Watters, A. E. (1989). *Reasoned/intuitive action: An individual difference moderator of the attitude-behavior relationship in the 1988 U. S. presidential election.* Unpublished master's thesis, Department of Psychology, University of Massachusetts at Amherst.

Weiner, B. (1985). A theory of motivation for some classroom experiences. *Journal of Educational Psychology, 71,* 3–25.

Wicker, A. W. (1969). Attitudes versus actions: The relationship of verbal and overt behavioral responses to attitude objectives. *Journal of Social Issues, 25,* 41–78.

Wortman, M. S. (1987). Entrepreneurship: An integrating typology and evaluation of the empirical research in the field. *Journal of Management, 13,* 259–277.

# Index

abilities, 26
  intellectual, 26
  social, 26
  verbal, 26
accounting, 101
affect, 12, 26, 59
Ajzen, theory of planned behav-
    ior, 3, 5, 9, 15, 27, 29-31,
    33, 35, 37, 40, 42, 52 63,
    90, 97-98, 106
artificial covariance, 102
assessments
  of availability of resources, 13,
    42, 46, 60, 92, 98, 106
  of constraints, 42, 46, 92
  of entrepreneurial self-efficacy,
    41, 48-49, 53, 68, 74, 79,
    81, 83, 85, 91-94, 100, 106
  definition of, 13
  measurement of, 61-62
  of probability of success, 42, 47,
    60
  of task requirements, 41, 46, 60,
    97-98
attitudes, 5, 23-27, 30, 35-36, 38,
    87, 89, 99

attitude-behavior, relationship, 26

background, of person, 2
behavior, 1-2, 5, 12, 15-17, 19-20,
    22, 24, 26-27, 31, 33, 36-
    37,     40, 42, 52, 58,
    87, 89, 99
  planned, 5
  *See also* entrepreneurial
    behavior
behavior approach to entrepreneurship, 1-2
beliefs, 23, 89
  cognitive, 26
birthday, traumatic, 50
business, definition of, 21
business plan, 11, 101

capital, 2
career choice, 37, 39
change, desire for, 61
child birth, 9, 34, 51, 93, 101
Chinese, attitude toward, 25
cognition, 25, 40, 43
common methods variance, 101,
    103, 107